THE **19** OF GREENE

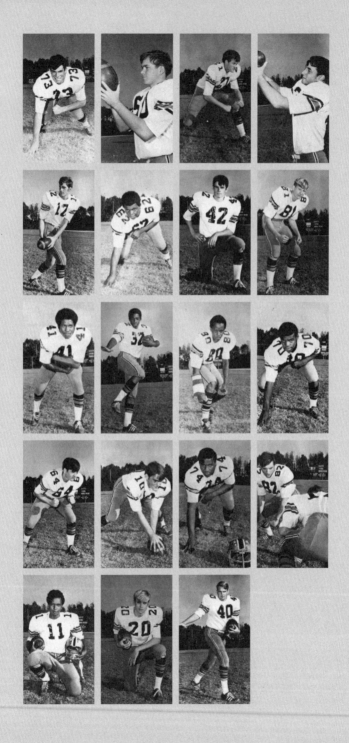

THE 19 OF GREENE

FOOTBALL, FRIENDSHIP, AND CHANGE IN THE FALL OF 1970

TONY BARNHART

The University of Georgia Press   Athens

Published by the University of Georgia Press
Athens, Georgia 30602
www.ugapress.org
© 2023 by Tony Barnhart
All rights reserved
Designed by Erin Kirk
Set in Miller Text, Sentinel, and Franklin Gothic
Printed and bound by Sheridan Books
The paper in this book meets the guidelines for
permanence and durability of the Committee on
Production Guidelines for Book Longevity of the
Council on Library Resources.

Most University of Georgia Press titles are
available from popular e-book vendors.

Printed in the United States of America
27   26   25   24   23   P   5   4   3   2   1

Library of Congress Control Number: 2023939009
ISBN 9780820365640 (paperback)
ISBN 9780820365657 (epub)
ISBN 9780820365664 (PDF)

To the players, students,

coaches, faculty, and administrators

of Greene County High School,

1970–1971

CONTENTS

FOREWORD CHARLES TURNER

I'm Charles Turner, and I graduated from Greene County High School in the class of 1971.

Before enrolling at Greene County High, I attended Floyd T. Corry High School, which was not very far away. For the most part, schools were segregated in Greene County and in many other areas of the South before the fall of 1970.

Greene County and Floyd T. Corry were so close to each other that the students could hear each other at recess. I'm 95 percent sure that one of the voices I heard across the way was that of Tony Barnhart. Little could I know at the time that we would one day become friends and teammates.

Dr. Martin Luther King Jr. was one of my role models, and he always preached that people should be judged by the content of their character rather than the color of their skin. I truly feel that Tony is one who believes as Dr. King did.

It was something new for me when I bused over to Greene County High with the other F. T. Corry players for spring practice in 1970. I had never even heard of spring practice. At Corry, it was football in the fall, basketball in the winter, and track in the spring. In the ninth grade, my mom wouldn't let me play football, even though Dad didn't care. Sophomore year was a bench-warming year, but by my junior year, I was a starter at wide receiver, catching four touchdown passes in one game.

In the spring of 1970, even though I was a bit nervous, I had confidence in my abilities, and everybody knew I had a strong arm. I hated playing quarterback, but everybody from Corry wanted me to go out for that position, even though my heart was set on being a receiver.

Our numbers were few (we had only nineteen players), and most of us had to play both offense and defense as well as special teams, but we thought we had the makings of a good team. However, after losing to the seniors in the spring game and then dropping our first two regular-season games in the fall, we weren't so sure.

But then we started to play with confidence.

We went on to win the rest of our regular-season games, except for one against Monroe Area, on a night when our team was plagued with cramps.

Every one of my teammates had a role in the success of our season. Even though we each had our own primary position we specialized in, we all had to play both ways since there were so few of us (and only sixteen of the nineteen actually played). But we had nine tough seniors.

Coach C. S. Veazey, Coach Larry Callair, Coach Mack Poss, Coach Nicholas Antone, Coach Nathaniel Whitehead, and Coach Dennis Fordham were very knowledgeable and tough. The administration was so supportive. I can remember our principal, Ellis Foster, would stop me in the hall and talk sports for a complete class period.

Eli Jackson, who was the principal at Corry and came to Greene County High as our associate principal, was extremely smart and loved the Tigers. I still remember his motto: "Manners will take you where money can't." I have used that advice quite often.

When Tony told me he was going to write a book about our 1970 team at Greene County, I was not surprised. I had tracked his career with the *Atlanta Journal-Constitution* as I started my career in education. I followed in the footsteps of my mom, who taught in Greene County for forty-three years.

Tony is the type of guy who doesn't meet a stranger. No one is too high or too low for him to carry on a conversation with them. That's evident in the fact he asked me to do the foreword to this book. There were many others whom he could have selected, so I feel honored, if unworthy.

I have accomplished quite a bit in my lifetime, for which my peers have honored me by inducting me into four different Halls of Fame. I also was mentioned in a book by Dr. J (Julius Erving), and a gym at Cedar Shoals High School in Athens, Georgia, has my name on it. This opportunity ranks up there with all of them. Thanks, Tony, you're the best!!!

CHARLES TURNER graduated from Greene County High School in 1971 and attended Clark College (now Clark Atlanta University) on a football scholarship. After a free-agent tryout with the Dallas Cowboys, Turner began a career in coaching and athletics administration. He is in the Halls of Fame of Clark Atlanta University, Cedar Shoals High School, the City of Athens, and the Georgia Athletic Directors Association. He lives in Statham, Georgia, with his wife, Cynthia. They have three adult children and six grandchildren.

PROLOGUE BILL CURRY *A Quiet Redemption*

"By now the black-and-white photo was a bit wrinkled, but the faces of the players were forever young. They were dressed out in their football finest . . . for a team picture . . . in the school yearbook. . . . [But this] was not just any football team. . . . This was the Greene County Tigers of 1970."

Football, with its obvious flaws, remains the only game of which I am aware in which every player needs every teammate on every play to have a chance to excel. Football players need a teammate to pull their jerseys over their pads. For gosh sakes, we can't even get dressed without each other! The practices are unbelievably hot (or freezing cold), muddy and inundated (or dry), long and demanding beyond description.

What keeps us and men like Tony Barnhart and his Greene County teammates out there? Why not just quit such a painful, foolish enterprise? The answer is not simple, but it always contains this truth: we are much more alike than we are different. Oh, and we love football!

Those who have been taught by our culture to hate one another begin to love, and it feels good. We stand by each other in the fourth quarter, we win or lose together . . . we learn to love one another.

What I had learned in Green Bay, Wisconsin, in 1965, five years before Tony and his teammates learned it in Greene County,

Bill Curry, who played on Super Bowl teams at Green Bay and Baltimore, is seen here with Tony on a trip to Notre Dame. Photo courtesy of the National Football Foundation.

Georgia, was that the absence of prejudice is fundamental to a winning team, or to *any* kind of team. Vince Lombardi would not tolerate racism, and I had never been in a huddle with an African American . . . ever. Other NFL teams refused to integrate, and yet Lombardi refused to relent in his open policy. Not coincidentally, nobody could beat us.

That unlikely bunch of nineteen black and white Northeast Georgia kids steeled themselves, did their homework, and then did the totally unfair job of ignoring the hatred surrounding them while putting in the work every day of that magical 1970 season.

In the process they discovered the "Miracle of Team."

Think about it. The fifty-cent word is *synergism*, but Tony writes it far better: "We were a team of black men and white men for which the whole—in football and in life—was so much greater than the sum of its parts. . . . And brothers and sisters, it doesn't get any better than that."

Quietly, they loved, were loved, and were somehow redeemed . . . without fanfare, till the shocking ending (a championship!).

It was Quiet Redemption at its best . . . the kind that changes lives . . . the kind that changes the world, to this very day.

BILL CURRY played football for Bobby Dodd at Georgia Tech and then played in the NFL for ten seasons, appearing in Super Bowls with the Green Bay Packers and the Baltimore Colts. He also was the head football coach at Georgia Tech (1980–1986), the University of Alabama (1987–1989), the University of Kentucky (1990–1996), and Georgia State University (2008–2012). He is a member of the Georgia Tech Sports Hall of Fame and the Georgia Sports Hall of Fame.

ACKNOWLEDGMENTS

This is my sixth book, and it was by far the most rewarding to write. That's because it gave me the chance to reunite with my teammates, coaches, and teachers at Greene County High School, most of whom I had neither seen nor spoken to in fifty years. It was a wonderful opportunity to reflect on my life and career that very few people get.

So the first round of thanks goes to my teammates, coaches, and teachers for their help with and support of this project.

Many thanks also to my English teacher and friend Tommi Ward, who was the first person I interviewed for the book. She was the one who encouraged me to become a writer more than fifty years ago.

Thanks to Carey Williams, the longtime editor, publisher, and owner of the *Herald-Journal* newspaper in Greensboro, Georgia. He was very enthusiastic about this project and opened his archives to me. "Mr. Carey" has been incredibly supportive throughout my career, and I am grateful.

A big thanks to Becky Taylor of the *Tifton (Georgia) Gazette*, who shared a treasure trove of newspaper articles about Greene County dating back to the 1940s. It was an incredible source of information.

Thanks to Nicole Chillemi of Festival Hall in Greensboro. She opened her doors and gave me a home base when I was in Greensboro to conduct interviews.

Thanks to Dr. Nate Holly of the University of Georgia Press. This is the first time I've worked with an academic publishing house, and Dr. Holly helped me navigate the process.

Thanks as well to UGA Press staff editor Jon Davies and my copyeditor Arthur Johnson. Because of their efforts, we have a much better book, and I appreciate that.

I had a lot of help tracking down all my teammates. Especially helpful in this area were Nicholas Antone, our coach and English teacher; and Charles Turner, our quarterback, and my friend for over fifty years.

Thanks to my friend and photographer extraordinaire Rob Saye. Charles and I visited Greene County on February 23, 2022, and Rob was there to capture some incredible memories.

Thanks as well to Beth Lyon, who shared some very important photos from when Charles was inducted into the Greene County Tigers Ring of Honor.

Much love and many thanks to my mom, Sara Lord, who taught me to love reading and writing at a very early age. She has been a constant source of love and support from the day she brought me into this world.

Thanks to my brother, David, who was my first competitor in sports and who has been a big supporter throughout my career. He was also a teammate on the 1970 Greene County team. I love you.

My wife, Maria, and I met as students at Greene County High School fifty-four years ago. We celebrated our forty-fifth wedding anniversary on August 14, 2022. She has always been my rock and the glue that holds our family together. Any success that I have achieved is because of Maria's constant love and support.

I also want to thank my daughter, Sara, who has always encouraged me and made me proud to be her dad.

Finally, Maria and I want to thank all our friends and family who still live in Greene County. Every time we come back to visit, they embrace us, and we truly appreciate it. For us, Greene County will always be home.

I hope you enjoy the book.

THE 19 OF GREENE

INTRODUCTION

This incredible journey started the day I went through an envelope of old photographs given me by my mother.

Knowing my bad habits, my wife, Maria, had written "PHOTOS! DO NOT DESTROY!" on the outside of the envelope.

With that not-so-gentle warning in mind, I carefully rummaged through the envelope's contents, which included photos of such disparate things as Boy Scout meetings (Troop 306), Little League baseball games, and snowball fights with my younger brother, David.

And there it was.

By now the black-and-white photo was a bit wrinkled, but the faces of the players were forever young. They were dressed out in their football finest, posing for a team picture that would appear in the school yearbook. With the players were three coaches: head coach C. S. Veazey and assistants Mack Poss and Larry Callair.

The joyful memories came rushing back.

This was not just any high school football team. No sir. This was the Greene County Tigers of 1970.

This team was special, and not because it won a division championship and played for a region championship despite having only nineteen (that's right, nineteen) players on its roster.

No, this team will always be remembered and revered because, for the first time in school history, black students and white students played football together.

I was a senior on the 1970 team, and I can attest that none of us ever thought of ourselves as trailblazers. We were teenage boys who loved playing football. When the players from predominately black Floyd T. Corry High School made the short bus ride over to predominately white Greene County High School for that first practice in the spring of 1970, no one considered the broader societal implications of what we were about to do.

We just wanted to win. And if combining the talent of the two schools gave us a better chance to win more games, then so be it.

"It never occurred to any of us that we were doing anything special," said Charles Turner, our African American quarterback, who came from Corry High. "We just wanted to play ball. And we wanted to win."

For the nineteen players on that team, any reflection on the deeper meaning of what happened in the fall of 1970 at Greene County High School would have to wait until later in life.

That time has arrived.

The COVID-plagued 2020 football season marked the fiftieth anniversary of the 19 of Greene. We didn't get to celebrate in person. More on that later.

Fifteen of us are still living.

My goal with this book was to talk with the other fourteen guys to get their version of the 1970 season, an experience that none of us will ever forget. I interviewed them all—twelve of them in person.

I did these interviews fully understanding that everybody would remember things a little differently, especially now that we're more than fifty years removed from the actual events.

I also knew that race would be an inescapable part of this story. I look back at these events through the prism and experience of a sixty-nine-year-old white man. Charles Turner, who remains my friend to this day, was a black quarterback on a team that was integrated for the first time. The experience was not easy for him. There was pressure from people who wanted to see him fail. There was also pressure from a black community that desperately wanted him to succeed.

Our coaches were asked to do something that had never been done before in Greene County. No one knew how—or if—it was going to work. There was no road map or instruction manual to guide us through what happened that fall.

We knew that not everyone agreed with the idea of black children and white children going to school together, much less playing football together.

Some white families took their children out of the public school system and enrolled them at the newly created Nathanael Greene Academy, one of hundreds of private schools that sprang up throughout the South when integration became the law of the land.

After Greene County lost its first two games in the fall of 1970, our team and our season could easily have gone off the rails.

But neither did. We came back and won seven of our next eight to reach our region championship game.

"Our team bonded pretty quickly, and when things got tough we held it together," said Dene Channell, our fullback/linebacker, who had played quarterback at Greene County High the season before. "Our coaches were not going to let us come apart."

I would have loved to have been able to talk with our head coach, C. S. Veazey, about the difficulties of managing our team through that unforgettable season, but he died in 2011. However, I did talk with his son, Chartie, who was a manager on the team, and his daughter Lynn.

I was able to visit with the four living assistant coaches at their homes. Mack Poss and Dennis Fordham were already at Greene County High when consolidation took place, while Nicholas Antone and Larry Callair joined the staff from Corry. Two other coaches who came over from Corry, Nathaniel Whitehead and Benny Asbury, had passed away by the time I began working on this book.

Coach Poss now lives in Toccoa, where he moved after the 1970 season to join Coach Veazey at Stephens County High School. I spent most of a day with him and his wife, Janice.

In October 2019, I went with Charles Turner and another former teammate, Ben Allen Gresham, to see Coach Callair in Augusta, about two hours east of Atlanta. Due to a lawn mower accident in April 2019, this once-powerful man, who had played semi-pro football to supplement his income as a coach and teacher, was confined to a wheelchair. He was thrilled that his former players would come to see him. That was a special day. Coach Callair passed away on January 8, 2023.

Mr. Antone still lives in Greene County. I visited him and his wife, Joan, at their home in Greensboro.

Coach Fordham went back to the University of Georgia after the 1970–1971 school year to pursue his doctorate in math education. From there, he launched a long and distinguished career in school administration and eventually became the superintendent of the Hall County, Georgia, school system. I visited him and his wife, Andrea, at their home in Covington, Georgia, about forty minutes east of Atlanta.

So many other voices deserve to play a part in telling this story. Tommi Ward was a young English teacher who played a very significant role in the integration of the two schools. She and another English teacher, the aforementioned Mr. Antone, laid some important groundwork in the fall of 1969 that helped smooth the way for the following school year. Details of what they did are included in chapter 3.

Our principal, Ellis Foster, had perhaps the toughest job of all. His calm, measured demeanor and leadership skills under difficult circumstances were very much needed in that first year. Mr. Foster died in 2008, but I had a chance to talk to his daughter, Kathie, about the special challenges of the 1970–1971 school year.

"I will always remember Mr. Foster talking to the entire faculty—black and white—as we were getting ready for the year," said Coach Poss, who in addition to his coaching duties taught physical education and driver's education.

"He said, 'Do what you were called to do. Be a professional.

"'You were called to teach. Teach them.'"

This is a story about football, politics, and social change, which have always been a tension-filled mix, particularly in the South.

Ultimately, this is a story about how nineteen teenagers (twelve white, seven black) from different backgrounds formed a team that would rally a school, a town, and a county that were more than a little uncertain whether integration would truly work.

It worked because it had to. It worked because it was the right thing to do. But I am convinced—and my teammates and coaches remain convinced—that there were fewer critics of the integration of Greene County High School because of the 19 of Greene.

At the end of the day, I wanted this book to be about the players: the four whom we've lost—Edward Stapleton, Freddie Walker, James Kimbro, and James Scott—and the fifteen who are still here to share their memories.

The interviews with my former teammates were joyful. As we talked, we kept coming back to the same thought: "Can you believe it's been fifty years?"

When I look at the team photo today, I see nineteen incredibly young faces who were challenged by our coaches and teachers to believe in something bigger than ourselves. That is not an easy thing for a teenager to do.

"This was one of those things that you don't really appreciate until later in your life," said Tom Faust, an end at Greene County in 1970 and 1971. "You just don't understand the importance of it while it is happening."

Now we do. And some fifty-two years later we can say that what the 19 of Greene accomplished in the fall of 1970 has stood the test of time.

This is their story.

1

GOING HOME TO GREENE

Fifty years. Yep. Almost fifty-two, to be exact.

It was February 23, 2022, and that's how much time had passed since Charles Turner and I last stood at the fifty-yard line at Greene County High School's Tiger Stadium.

The last time we had been together in this special place was November 13, 1970, the night Greene County beat Morgan County 28–6 for the Region 8-AA East Division football championship.

It was the first football championship of any kind that Greene County had won since 1956. But that is not what made that night special. What made it special was the fact that we won our division with the first integrated football team in our school's history.

Much has changed in the half century since.

Charles went on to play quarterback at Clark College (now Clark Atlanta University), an HBCU (historically black college or university). After a brief tryout with the Dallas Cowboys, he became a high school coach and administrator. As a coach, Charles won a state championship in girls' basketball.

I went on to have a career as a sportswriter and broadcaster for newspapers, radio, and television. In 1998 I was named to the Football Writers Association Hall of Fame. I was inducted into the Georgia Sports Hall of Fame in May 2021.

The irony of this day was that we both grew up in Union Point, a suburb of Greensboro, about seven miles away from Tiger Stadium. Our homes were but a few miles apart.

But we didn't meet until the spring of 1970, when my school, Greene County High, and his school, Floyd T. Corry High, merged to create the first fully integrated school in our county's history.

With this book nearing its completion, I still felt there was a missing piece to the story. So I picked up the phone and called Charles.

"You up for a trip down memory lane?" I asked.

"Absolutely," he said.

I picked Charles up at his home in Statham, Georgia, just outside of Athens, and we headed straight for Greensboro, about forty miles away.

Growing up, Charles and I had a lot in common. His father, Charlie, worked in his own floor-finishing business until he retired. My dad, Bobby, ran his own construction business. Charles's mother, Chloe, was an educator for forty-three years. My mother, Sara, worked in various capacities at Chipman-Union Manufacturing, the textile mill and primary employer in Union Point.

Charles and I both had a small-town, middle-class upbringing. From an early age, our parents taught us the virtues of hard work and treating others with respect. Those values would serve us well as we grew up and left Greene County in 1971 to pursue our dreams.

But our experiences growing up in Greene County were very different in one important aspect.

Charles is black.

I am white.

"There are things you want to remember," said Charles when we talked about his upbringing. "But there are other things you want to forget."

A BRIEF HISTORY OF GREENE COUNTY

Nathanael Greene was a major general in the Continental Army during the American Revolutionary War. He emerged from the war with a reputation as one of George Washington's best and most capable officers.

Greene's Continental troops outmaneuvered a numerically superior British force under the command of General Charles Cornwallis and won several battles that helped loosen British control of the American South. After the war Greene became a farmer, but his crops, for the most part, failed.

On February 3, 1786, the Georgia legislature named a tract of land in the east-central portion of the state "Greene County" in his honor. At the time it was one of just 11 counties in Georgia. Today the state has 159 counties; only Texas (254) has more.

Nathanael Greene died on June 19, 1786, just twenty-three days away from his forty-fourth birthday.

The town of Greensboro, also named for Greene, was founded in 1786 as the county seat. The other communities in Greene County included Union Point, Siloam, Woodville, White Plains, and Penfield.

Like many small Georgia towns founded around the turn of the eighteenth century, Greensboro was built on a cotton-based economy that made a handful of people rich but relied on the labor of poor whites and enslaved blacks in order to thrive. By the 1830s, Greene County was producing one of the largest cotton crops of any county in Georgia.

According to the *New Georgia Encyclopedia*, the end of the Civil War unleashed pent-up social forces in Greensboro and Greene County. Newly emancipated black people migrated to Greensboro and built a community known as Canaan, which still exists today. African Americans were able to build a power base in 1868 by using their votes to elect a slate of Republican candidates.

But then came a white backlash fueled by the Ku Klux Klan that reclaimed power for whites in Greene County through a series of beatings, home burnings, and murders. The residents of

Canaan formed a militia and fought back. But by 1874 the black power structure had been removed.

Growing up in Greene County, Charles and I were both aware of local restaurants where black patrons were unwelcome or were asked to sit at the back of the building. The irony was that those same restaurants would eventually host the integrated Greene County football team for its pregame meals during the 1970 season.

"That was a big deal," said Charles.

There were segregated water fountains labeled WHITE and COLORED, a practice that the Civil Rights Act of 1964 finally outlawed.

Each movie theater in Union Point and Greensboro had a separate entrance for black patrons, who had to walk up two flights of stairs outside the back of the building to enter and sat segregated in the balcony. They would exit the same way without ever coming into direct contact with a white person.

When I was young, it never occurred to me that this was morally wrong. And no one in my family ever talked about it. This was just the way it was supposed to be. At least that's what we told ourselves back then.

I remember a black man who worked for my father—his name was Sam—coming to our back door on a Saturday morning. Sam asked to see my dad, and I said, "Yes sir."

After Sam had left, my father corrected me.

"Don't call him 'sir,'" he said, with an edge to his voice. He didn't say why. But I knew why.

My mother had two young sons and a husband who worked outdoors every day in the construction business. She was working full time outside the home herself and needed help with laundry and ironing. I remember riding in the car with her and stopping at a modest home on the Washington Highway just a few miles from our home. A black woman came out of the house with a large basket of newly ironed clothes. She and my mother exchanged only a few words before my mother quickly reached into her purse for a few dollars.

"Thank you, Miss Sara," the black lady said.

"See you next week," my mother said.

The point of these two stories is that my only interaction with African American people at that time in my life was to see them in a service capacity to whites.

It really wasn't until a few black students came to Greene County High from Floyd T. Corry in the late 1960s that I had any meaningful interaction with African Americans my age. Then it became clear that their experience of growing up in Greene County was very different from mine.

"It was a separate but unequal society," Charles said. "The whole idea of separate but equal was a joke. It was part of our culture.

"But things got better."

Yes, things did get better in Greene County, but not before there was change—seismic change.

And this change did not come easily. Not by a long shot.

NOT MUCH FOR YOUNG PEOPLE TO DO

As in most small towns in Georgia, there wasn't a whole lot for the young people of Greene County—black or white—to do in the 1950s and 1960s. Athens, the home of the University of Georgia, was thirty minutes away, and most of the time that's where you would take a date.

Charles and I were in different schools, but we both were tied up with sports: football in the fall and basketball in the winter. In the spring, I played tennis and he ran track. In the summer we both worked to earn some money for the next school year.

Charles and his classmates at Corry High School would hang out at Love Joy Jackson's Grocery Store.

"They sold coconut cookies for a penny," he said.

My friends would hang out at Jimmy Smith's Dairy Bar in Union Point, the first fast-food place I can remember.

Another gathering place for my friends was Hunter's Drug Store at the corner of Main Street and Broad Street in downtown

Greensboro. The store had a soda fountain that served what became known as an EHB—"Empty Hotdog Bun." It included everything you would put on a hot dog—mustard, ketchup, onions, relish—everything *except* the hot dog. And the bun was toasted.

The reality of growing up in Greene County was that black students and white students did not meaningfully interact with one another until the schools merged in the fall of 1970.

"A LOT OF GREAT MEMORIES"

So here Charles and I were, in Greensboro and headed back to Greene County High School, where we had first met in the spring of 1970. We had some time before our first appointment, so we decided to stop by Charles's former school, Floyd T. Corry High. The school was originally built in 1950 in response to a series of petitions from black citizens of Greene County and twenty-eight other Georgia counties to improve schools that had fallen into disrepair. In September 1956 the school was named for Floyd T. Corry, the former Greene County school superintendent, who had been killed in an automobile accident the previous November.

Unfortunately, when Charles and I got there, the school was fenced off and in the process of being torn down to make room for another building. As of this writing, it has not been determined what the new building will be. We parked and got out to take a closer look at a piece of history that was being dismantled before our eyes.

The building in front of us had actually contained both Floyd T. Corry Primary (grades 1–3) and Floyd T. Corry High (grades 8–12).

Not far away was Floyd T. Corry Elementary (grades 4–7), on the hill near the gas pumps that would be used to refill all the Greene County school buses each day.

Charles spent eleven of his first twelve years of education in those three schools. His senior year, of course, was at Greene County High School.

Charles's mother, Chloe, taught at F. T. Corry Primary School, and he remembered riding with her to school each day.

When Charles was younger, she would drop him off at F. T. Corry Elementary in the morning, and at the end of the day he would walk back past Love Joy Jackson's to the primary school and catch a ride home with his mom.

As a student and football player at Floyd T. Corry High School, Charles would walk a route past Love Joy Jackson's all the way to Robinson Field, where his team practiced and played its games. His parents would pick him up at the field after practice.

So Monday through Thursday during football season the players would walk from Floyd T. Corry High School to Robinson Field to practice.

"But on game day we rode the bus," he said with a smile.

It was a lot to take in. I thought I sensed some sadness in his voice and said so.

Not really, he said.

"There are a lot of great memories there," said Charles, looking at the remnants of the school. "But life moves on. I know there are people who don't like to see things torn down. But as long as whatever you put back is better, I don't have a problem with it."

THE "NEW" GREENE COUNTY HIGH SCHOOL

Then it was on to Greene County High School. The building where we attended classes our senior year is now home to the offices for the county school system. We would see that building later in the day.

In 1982 the county built a new Greene County High School. I parked my car, and we walked inside.

There to greet us as we walked in was Eddie Hood, who had left Central Gwinnett High School in June 2021 to become the director of athletics at Greene County High School and was subsequently appointed the school's associate principal. A native of Snellville, Georgia, Mr. Hood was named the Region 8-AAAAAA

Athletic Director of the Year by the Georgia Athletic Directors Association (GADA) in his last year at Central Gwinnett.

Mr. Hood has a lot in common with Charles, who was a very successful athletic director at Cedar Shoals High School in Athens and is a member of the GADA Hall of Fame. During our visit we learned that Mr. Hood was soon to become the principal at Greene County High School, replacing James Peek, who would be retiring in May 2022.

In December 2021, Mr. Hood hired Terrance Banks as the new head football coach at Greene County High School. Coach Banks had been the head coach at Meadow Creek High School in Norcross, Georgia, and at several other schools before being hired at Greene County.

The Greene County High football team had struggled the previous three seasons, going 2–8 in 2019, 1–8 in 2020, and 4–6 in 2021. Coach Larry Milligan, who was in his second tour of duty at Greene County, announced his retirement in late November 2021.

While things have not gone well on the field in recent years, Greene County football is not a stranger to winning. The Tigers won a state championship under Charlie Winslette in 1993 and reached the state championship game under Coach Milligan in 2005.

In the six years previous, Coach Banks pointed out, Greene County had won nine games in a season twice (2016, 2018).

Tiger Stadium, just a short walk from the school, was built in 1965 when Greensboro High School and Union Point High School—both white—merged to form Greene County High. Back then there was a small field house, a press box, bleachers, lights, and an electronic scoreboard; a dirt track encircled the playing field. The cost to build the stadium was $50,000. That was a lot of money in 1965.

Today Tiger Stadium is one of the nicest stadiums of its size that you'll find in Georgia. It boasts a state-of-the-art artificial playing surface, a beautiful track, and an updated press box and bleachers.

Charles and I were both impressed.

Mr. Hood and Coach Banks took us inside the stadium, where we were joined by Dr. Chris Houston, superintendent of the Greene County School System. Before becoming the superintendent of schools, he was the sheriff of Greene County for almost two decades. Rob Saye, a professional photographer and long-time friend, also joined us. Rob understood how important this trip was for Charles and me and agreed to be a part of it.

Charles and I walked to midfield and looked around us. The stadium was empty and eerily quiet. But as we talked it was easy to remember when it was full and loud—very loud. The Tigers played six home games in the fall of 1970 and won all but one—a 24–21 loss to Monroe Area High School. We finished strong, beating Madison County and Morgan County in Tiger Stadium to clinch the division championship. (Chapter 6 has a complete summary of all eleven of our games.)

After a while, Charles and I decided to take one last lap around Tiger Stadium and just let the memories wash over us. The only thing that would have made it better was if our teammates and coaches could have taken the lap with us.

Then we walked into the stands and sat for a few moments.

"I still can't believe it's been fifty years," Charles said.

Then came the very special part of our visit home.

We asked if we could walk the halls of the old Greene County High School building, which were such a mass of sound and energy when classes were changing.

But before we went into the building, we were joined by two of our former teachers, Tommi Ward and Nicholas Antone. Both taught English, and both played pivotal roles in the 1970–1971 school year, the year the schools were completely integrated. (You'll get the entire story of Mrs. Ward and Mr. Antone in chapter 3.) Mr. Antone's wife, Joan, was also kind enough to join us for some photos outside the main entrance to the school.

Dr. Houston and Russell Brock, the executive director of human resources and student services for the Greene County School System, took us on a tour of the building. The classrooms had been transformed into offices. But we vividly remembered where Mrs. Ward's and Mr. Antone's classrooms were located. I had social studies with William Nesbit in the last room on the hall, before the door that led to the back parking lot.

I remember that Mr. Nesbit, my first black teacher, gave us each an assignment of bringing something from home that represented the popular culture. I brought a record album by Steppenwolf and played a track called "The Pusher." The refrain went: "God damn the pusher."

Mr. Nesbit liked it. My mother, as you might imagine, hated it. Charles and I felt like we were eighteen again.

We finished our tour in the old Greene County High gymnasium, where Charles, Al Cason, Dene Channell, Eric Ashley, Mike Jackson, Kenny Cato, and many others lit it up on a regular basis during basketball season.

After saying our thanks to everyone, we headed down U.S. Route 278 to Union Point, about seven miles away.

Tony and Charles with their former teachers Nicholas Antone and Tommi Ward when they visited Greene County on February 23, 2022. Also pictured is Joan Antone, Mr. Antone's wife. Photo courtesy of Rob Saye.

Tony and Charles sit in the bleachers at Tiger Stadium during their visit to
Greene County High School on February 23, 2022. Photo courtesy of Rob Saye.

A couple of miles outside Union Point we stopped to see Charles's family home. His parents had been gone for a while, but he'd used the past few months to work on the house and get it ready for sale.

Then we headed into town. We passed Al Cason's house and remembered that just across the road was Whit's Grill, a motel and truck stop. This was before Interstate 20 connected Atlanta and Augusta, so a lot of truckers stopped to spend the night at Whit's Grill. Things changed considerably when I-20 was completed in the late 1970s.

Al remembers that he and his sister Louise could go across the road to play at Kathy Whitley's house. Kathy's dad, Harold, owned Whit's Grill.

"But we were not allowed to go in the grill," Al told me.

Union Point got its name because several rail lines intersected there. Many traveling salesmen would use Union Point as a place of rest along their journeys. When Charles and I graduated from Greene County High in 1971, Union Point had a population of 1,624. The latest census figures have the town's population at 1,594.

Our first stop in Union Point was the Siloam Missionary Baptist Church, Charles's home church. His parents' funerals were held there.

Then we went to the First United Methodist Church of Union Point, which was a big part of growing up for my brother and me.

Next, I took Charles and Rob on a minitour of Union Point. My family lived in several places in Union Point when I was growing up. The last house we lived in before I headed off to college was at 405 Veazey Street. My father, Bobby, built it in the late 1960s. My parents got divorced in the early 1970s, and the house was put up for sale. My dad died in 1999. My mom— ninety years old as of December 23, 2022—now lives in Greensboro.

Last, we went to downtown Union Point, which has not changed significantly since I was a boy. Rhodes Sports Corner, which is owned by Union Point mayor Lanier Rhodes, still holds its valuable corner spot.

We passed the building that once was Union Point's movie theater. There was a time when the theater reserved its main entrance at the front for "Whites" and had a "Colored" entrance in the back.

We drove back to Greene County High School and dropped Rob at his car.

After a late lunch out by I-20, Charles and I headed back to Statham to put a wrap on this very special day. And inevitably the conversation turned to the journey of the past fifty-two years and how we got to this point in time.

Bottom line: The past half century had been a helluva ride for us both. And many others had worked and sacrificed a lot so that we—a white man and a black man now in our late sixties—could celebrate this journey together in 2022.

It all started in 1954, the year after I was born.

2

"WITH ALL DELIBERATE SPEED"

On May 17, 1954, the United States Supreme Court unanimously ruled in *Brown v. Board of Education of Topeka* that the segregation of children by race in educational opportunities was a violation of the U.S. Constitution. More simply put by Chief Justice Earl Warren: "Separate educational facilities are inherently unequal."

A year later, in *Brown v. Board of Education II*, the Court gave the states a road map and ordered that schools integrate "with all deliberate speed."

But many schools, particularly those in the Deep South, did *not* integrate with deliberate speed.

Led by politicians who saw the Supreme Court ruling as an infringement on states' rights by an overreaching federal government, the resistance to desegregation in the South was strong, and what little compliance that did take place occurred at a snail's pace.

In 1956, nineteen U.S. senators and eighty-two members of Congress, representing all the states of the former Confederacy, issued "The Southern Manifesto: A Declaration of Constitutional Principles." This resolution denounced the *Brown* decision and proclaimed that the signatories would use "all lawful means to bring about a reversal of this decision which is contrary to the Constitution."

The Manifesto further stated that the *Brown* decision was "destroying the amicable relations between the white and Negro races that have been created through 90 years of patient effort by the good people of both races."

In 1958, Ernest Vandiver ran a successful campaign for governor of Georgia on a platform of fiscal conservatism while promising to defend segregation. His campaign pledge was "No, not one," an abridgment of his vow that no black children would sit in a classroom with white children in the state of Georgia.

Later in life, Vandiver would recant that pledge.

In 1961, a federal judge ordered the University of Georgia to integrate by admitting African American students Hamilton Holmes and Charlayne Hunter. At the encouragement of Atlanta business leaders such as future mayor Ivan Allen Jr., Vandiver chose not to defy the judge's ruling, breaking ranks with other segregationist southern governors, such as George Wallace of Alabama and Ross Barnett of Mississippi, who openly flouted such orders.

The passage of the Civil Rights Act of 1964, the enforcement of which would be handled by the U.S. Justice Department, began to accelerate the process of desegregation.

So it was no longer a question of if but when the counties of Georgia would ultimately comply with the federal mandate to desegregate the schools.

Until 1964, Greene County had three high schools in its educational system: predominately black Floyd T. Corry High School in Greensboro, and two white high schools in Greensboro and Union Point.

Greene County High School was formed in the fall of 1965 when the two white schools merged. The new school would be in Greensboro, but the decision to locate it there did not happen without a fight.

A long, bitter fight.

THE BATTLE BETWEEN UNION POINT AND GREENSBORO

As early as 1953, the Greene County Board of Education was coming under significant pressure from the state to consolidate the two white high schools in Greensboro and Union Point, located about seven miles apart. The state was about to embark on a program to upgrade school facilities throughout Georgia and wanted nearby schools to merge in order to be more cost efficient in these upgrades.

The Greene County Board of Education had already voted 3–2 to build one new high school to serve both communities.

But Union Point steadfastly refused to give up its school.

"The rivalry between Union Point and Greensboro was very serious and very emotional," said Lanier Rhodes, a lifelong resident of Union Point who today serves as its mayor. "If you lived in Union Point, you did not date somebody who lived in Greensboro. You just didn't do it."

"It was pretty clear to me that I couldn't date a boy from Greensboro," said Millie Yearwood Smith, who grew up in Union Point. "There was no discussion." (Note: Millie is my cousin.)

On September 29, 1953, the Crawfordville *Advocate-Democrat* reported that more than eight hundred Union Point residents had met to take part in a straw poll on whether to secede from Greene County and join nearby Taliaferro County, whose county seat was Crawfordville. The Taliaferro County line is only five miles east of Union Point.

According to the newspaper, the vote was 770 to 32 in favor of secession.

Mayor Ralph Rhodes, the father of Lanier Rhodes, told the Associated Press that the straw poll was conducted only after "many appeals" to the Greene County Board of Education: "We feel like we have been grossly discriminated against."

Dr. H. L. Cheves, a Union Point resident who spoke at the meeting, said, "If we cannot keep our high school in Greene County we will keep it in Taliaferro County."

Union Point did not secede from Greene County, but the battle over retaining its high school continued.

On February 9, 1955, the *Atlanta Constitution* reported that a delegation of more than three hundred Union Point residents would travel to Atlanta that day to meet with new governor Marvin Griffin to discuss the issue. According to the newspaper's report, the textile mill in Union Point, the town's primary employer, would close for the day so its employees could take part in the caravan, which would be led by Mayor Rhodes.

The next day, the *Constitution* reported that the caravan from Union Point to the Georgia State Capitol comprised more than five hundred people in eighty-one cars.

"We closed the town tight," Mayor Rhodes told reporter Jack Nelson, who was in his second year with the *Constitution* and would win a Pulitzer Prize for reporting in 1960. Nelson later served as the longtime, award-winning Washington bureau chief of the *Los Angeles Times*.

Sitting on the steps of the Capitol building while the meeting took place was Mayor Rhodes's five-year-old son, Lanier, and his sister Terri, who was seven.

"My dad and all those folks from Union Point were determined that they were going to do whatever it took to keep our high school," said Lanier Rhodes. "I will never forget it."

According to the *Herald-Journal* of Greensboro, on February 16, 1955, the Greene County Board of Education met and resolved "that the consolidation of white high schools in Greene County is not in the best interests of the children of Greene County nor of the citizens."

Union Point High School would continue, and the controversy would take another ten years to resolve.

In May 1964, the *Augusta Chronicle* reported that the Georgia State Board of Education had given the Greene County Board of Education an ultimatum that "some accepted consolidation" of its schools must be put into operation no later than 1965 or else state funds would be withheld.

The board further stated that it was "not going to take any action to require consolidation of Union Point High School with the Greensboro High School this year, with the hope that a satisfactory solution to the matter may be worked out in your interim period."

On September 3, 1965, Greensboro High School and Union Point High School officially consolidated, and Greene County High School opened its doors, ending the twelve-year struggle to get the two white schools under the same roof.

At the final Union Point High School graduation in the spring of 1965, diplomas were awarded in alphabetical order. Accordingly, Millie Yearwood, my cousin, received the last-ever diploma from Union Point High School.

Only three boys from Union Point played on the first football team representing Greene County High School in the fall of 1965: Jimmy Scott, Tommy McDonald, and Lanier Rhodes.

Little did the officials at Greene County High School know that five years later it would be consolidating again.

HOW FLOYD T. CORRY HIGH SCHOOL BEGAN

When the high school for African American students was built in Greensboro in the 1950s, it was originally named Greene County High School. (The high school for white students was Greensboro High School.)

But in 1956 Greene County High School was renamed to honor Floyd T. Corry, who was the county's beloved superintendent of schools for nineteen years. Corry was killed in November 1955 when his pickup truck was struck by another driver. He was only fifty-six years old.

On September 14, 1956, the *Herald-Journal* reported that the eight hundred students at Floyd T. Corry had fully embraced the school's new name.

"Upon learning their school had been renamed, the students gave an applause of approval," the article said. "Needless to say they were conscious of the great man for whom their school had been justly named." Floyd T. Corry was white.

The school's principal, Eli J. Jackson, began his career in education in 1928 as the teacher and principal of a one-teacher school in Oglethorpe County, Georgia.

Mr. Jackson was known for his love of the students at Corry.

"Mr. Jackson was a father figure to all students," said Charles Turner, who came from Floyd T. Corry to Greene County for his senior year in 1970. "My family was close to him and Mrs. Jackson because my mom was a schoolteacher for forty-three years. He recruited her to be a teacher.

"Without Mr. Jackson there is no Floyd T. Corry. He was a very smart and a very caring man."

Throughout his years as principal at Corry, Mr. Jackson would confront many challenges. Not the least of which was the struggle to get Corry High School its own gymnasium.

THE FIGHT TO GET FLOYD T. CORRY A GYMNASIUM

Each of the white high schools in Union Point and Greensboro had its own gymnasium in which to play basketball and host other indoor events, but Corry did not. Corry had to play its basketball games outside, which made the games subject to inclement weather.

On November 9, 1962, the *Herald-Journal* reported that a delegation of black citizens had requested that the basketball team at Corry be allowed to use Greensboro High's gymnasium for five games and the Union Point High gymnasium for four games during the coming basketball season.

This request was made in advance of a bond referendum on January 12, 1963, that would raise $125,000 specifically for building a gymnasium for Floyd T. Corry. Two previous bond referendums addressing the issue had been defeated.

In a letter to the editor of the *Herald-Journal* on January 11, 1963, the Greene County Board of Education pleaded for the passage of the bond referendum and appealed to fundamental fairness:

> There are two gymnasiums for the white students of this county but none for the Negro students. They have had to hold their athletic games outdoors, subject to the weather; and often have had to call off their games at the last minute.
>
> The Board wants to provide equal facilities for all the students of this county and feels that the Negro students need this building and are entitled to it.

Further on in the letter, the BOE said that if the bond referendum did not pass and the gym was not built, it had only two options: "1—Discontinue all basketball games in the county or 2—Allow the Negro students to use the gyms at Greensboro and Union Point for their games."

In that same edition of the newspaper, Eli Jackson made his case for passing the referendum:

> Now Greene County must in fairness meet its challenge to Negro citizens. Many fair-minded citizens have stated they are in favor of the Negro schools being well equipped and having adequate facilities to educate their pupils physically, spiritually, and mentally.
>
> The fair-minded Christian people of Greene County have the responsibility of showing leadership in all worthwhile activities. You, as leaders, are on trial before our State, Nation, and the World in being fair to all the children of all the people.
>
> Please be fair. Vote for bonds for a Negro School gymnasium in Greene County.

The bond referendum was rejected by a margin of 216 votes —819 for and 1,035 against.

The following Monday a delegation of black citizens again requested that Floyd T. Corry be able to use the white school gymnasiums in Union Point and Greensboro to play its home basketball games. On Wednesday, January 30, 1963, representatives of both races and officials from around the state were part of an emotional meeting at the Greene County courthouse in which they sought to find a solution to getting a gymnasium built for

Floyd T. Corry. The meeting was covered by Bill Shipp, the state news editor of the *Atlanta Constitution*.

According to the report from Mr. Shipp, Atlanta attorney Donald L. Hollowell, representing the Georgia Teachers and Education Association, suggested that another bond referendum be held. And until a new gymnasium was built, Corry should be allowed to play in the county's two white high school facilities.

"The floors wouldn't mind one bit, the seats wouldn't mind one bit, and the lights wouldn't mind one bit if it were utilized co-operatively," Mr. Hollowell was quoted as saying in Shipp's story.

What Mr. Hollowell proposed did not come to pass. In fact, the issue of a gym for Corry did not get resolved until two and a half years later.

On August 27, 1965, notice was given in the *Herald-Journal* of a $350,000 bond referendum. The funds would be used to build gymnasiums and classrooms for both Floyd T. Corry and Greene County High School. The referendum would be held on September 29.

According to a report in the *Herald-Journal*, the referendum passed by 144 votes—1,442 for and 1,298 against. Floyd T. Corry High School would finally get its gymnasium.

But five years later, Corry's basketball players would be playing in the gym at Greene County High School.

HOW INTEGRATION BEGAN

After the passage of the Civil Rights Act of 1964, school systems came under increasing federal pressure to formulate a plan to desegregate schools at a much faster pace. Some submitted complete proposals for desegregation. A total of seventy counties in Georgia submitted "certificates of compliance" with the understanding that a formal plan to completely desegregate would come later. Greene County was among those counties, according to a story in the *Atlanta Constitution* on February 20, 1965.

In the 1965–1966 academic year, six African American students—Katrina Breeding, Juanita Brown, Terry Brown, Murray

Lee Dobbins, Gayron Wright, and Sharon Wright—left Floyd T. Corry and enrolled in the eighth grade at Greene County High School. Three other students from Corry—Essie Pierce, Bernice Reid, and Elsie Crawford—enrolled as juniors. All total, seventeen black students began attending the previously all-white school grades 1–12 in the fall of 1965, according to a report in the *Herald-Journal*.

Ford Boston, the Greene County superintendent of schools, received a letter from Francis Keppel, the U.S. commissioner of education, stating that the Greene County schools were in compliance based on the plan it had submitted: "On the basis of review of the plan, particularly for the provisions made for the school year 1965–66, I have determined that the plan is adequate to accomplish the purposes of the Act and the Regulation of the Department of Health, Education, and Welfare."

Moving forward, wrote Mr. Keppel, the Greene County schools would agree not to dismiss or demote any teacher, principal, or other staff member serving pupils because of race, color, or national origin. He added: "With the inclusion of the understanding described above, the plan provides a basis for the approval of applications and for the payment of federal financial assistance at this time."

Katrina Breeding and Juanita Brown would stay at Greene County High School for the next five years and graduate in the spring of 1970.

Ms. Breeding was the daughter of William Breeding, a longtime educator and leader within the black community of Greene County. Mr. Breeding spent forty years as a teacher and a coach and served as principal of the black elementary school.

As coach of the Floyd T. Corry High School girls' basketball team, Mr. Breeding won three state championships, in 1959, 1960, and 1962.

In 1979 President Jimmy Carter invited Mr. Breeding to Washington, D.C., to witness the signing of the bill that created the Department of Education.

Katrina Breeding had cousins in Birmingham who were active

in the movement to desegregate the schools, and she wanted to be involved in making a difference in Greene County. She also wanted her own stories to tell when the entire family got together for Thanksgiving.

"People assume that my parents made me go to Greene County High School," said Ms. Breeding, who would later graduate from Clark College in Atlanta, her father's alma mater, and the Howard University School of Law. Today she is back in Greensboro, practicing law. "But it was a choice that I made based on the activism on my side of the family."

THE RESISTANCE

For Ford Boston, who had been the Greene County school superintendent since 1955, it became clear in the 1960s that the days of completely segregated schools were coming to an end.

However, some members of the white community resisted integration. And some of that resistance was very vocal.

"Daddy would get phone calls late at night and early in the morning," his daughter, Elaine Boston Carsel, said. "I could hear them screaming over the phone. Some people would come to the front door. They were so ugly to Daddy. He was just following the rules. It was the law."

Dene Channell was the quarterback for Greene County High the year before it merged with Corry. His father, J. W. Channell, was on the Greene County Board of Education. Dene's mother, Dorothy, was a math teacher at Greene County High School.

"There was a lot of concern about what would happen, and my parents talked about sending me to Woodward Academy in Atlanta," Dene said. "But I didn't want to do that. I wanted to stay with my teammates."

The incremental approach to integration was done in the hope that the public would be more accepting by the time full integration came in the fall of 1970, and the strong negative feelings on both sides of the color line would have subsided.

"Sure, there was resistance, but not just white resistance," said

Tom Faust, a white student who was a junior in the fall of 1970. "You're moving everybody's cheese."

PRIVATE SCHOOL IS FORMED

In August 1969, the year before full integration, the educational dynamic in Greene County changed with the formation of a private school, Nathanael Greene Academy (NGA). NGA began with an enrollment of 189 in grades 1–12. Its first graduating class in the spring of 1970 had 5 students.

"It was a hard decision, but at the time I didn't see where I had a choice," said Lindy Copelan, who attended NGA for his senior year in 1969–1970. "It was just the thing to do."

Other white parents sent their children to Woodward Academy in Atlanta, over an hour's drive away.

In fact, both NGA and Woodward Academy advertised in Greensboro's *Herald-Journal*, seeking to add to their student bodies.

FREEDOM OF CHOICE

Many counties surrounding Greene also adopted a freedom of choice model for pupil assignment in 1965 or 1966. Before each school year, these counties sent letters to all resident families informing them that their children were free to choose where they wanted to go to school. By federal mandate, the desegregation plan, along with a school-preference form, was printed in the local newspaper. The desegregation plan stated that no choice would be denied for any reason other than overcrowding.

Morgan County, whose county seat of Madison was about twenty minutes west of Greensboro, adopted its freedom of choice plan in 1965, with students able to choose between the previously all-white Morgan County High School and all-black Pearl High School.

According to the April 14, 1966, edition of the *Madisonian* newspaper, three thousand families in Morgan County received letters outlining the freedom of choice plan. In the fall of 1966, five black students elected to leave Pearl High School and enroll at Morgan County High School.

By 1969, only 3.8 percent of black students had chosen to move from Pearl to Morgan County High School.

In December 1969, a three-judge panel in U.S. district court essentially ruled that Georgia high schools would have to be fully integrated by September 1970.

On August 20, 1970, the *Madisonian* ran the headline "Public Schools to Open Here Tuesday; New Era Begins."

TROUBLES IN HANCOCK COUNTY

Hancock County, just southeast of Greene County, had two public high schools: all-black Hancock Central High School and all-white Sparta High, both located in the county seat of Sparta. Hancock County had agreed to a freedom of choice plan in 1965. One black student enrolled at Sparta High in the fall of 1965.

John Hancock Academy, a private school, opened its doors in Sparta in August 1966.

In 1969, the year before the schools were supposed to merge, Hancock Central had 2,200 students and was almost exclusively black. Sparta High had 370 students, of whom all but 70 were white.

According to the September 5, 1969, edition of the *Sparta Ishmaelite* newspaper, a group of 200 students from Hancock Central marched to Sparta High and requested immediate enrollment under the freedom of choice plan. School officials denied the request and closed all public schools until September 15. Sparta High had to move its opening football game to Oglethorpe County High School.

There were protests and school boycotts. The Ku Klux Klan held a rally in Sparta.

After an emergency meeting of the board of education, ninety-two students and two faculty members were immediately transferred from Hancock Central to Sparta High. In December another ninety-two black students were moved to Sparta High, leaving a slight white majority among its student body.

Sparta High School closed its doors in 1973. Today Hancock Central has 243 students and is 97 percent black.

John Hancock Academy, which is completing its fifty-eighth year, has 126 students. According to the Private School Review website, 3 percent of those are students of color.

PUTNAM COUNTY HAD TWO BLACK GRADUATES IN 1967

On August 19, 1965, a headline on the front page of the *Eatonton Messenger* newspaper read: "Putnam School Desegregation Plan to Become Effective This Month." A freedom of choice school-preference form appeared alongside the story.

Putnam County High School in Eatonton began accepting students from predominately black Butler-Baker High School in the mid-1960s and had its first two African American graduates in 1967. Butler-Baker's 1961 valedictorian was Alice Walker, the author of *The Color Purple*. Butler-Baker's last graduating class was in the spring of 1970.

Putnam County founded a private school, the Gatewood School, in 1970.

TURBULENCE IN TALIAFERRO

Taliaferro County, whose county seat is Crawfordville, had a most turbulent time with desegregation.

Black students attended the Murden School, while white students attended Alexander Stephens Institute, which was named after the vice president of the Confederacy.

In 1965, rather than integrate Alexander Stephens Institute, county school officials placed 139 white students on buses to attend segregated Warren County High School and Greene County High School, which had 17 black students. Crawfordville police denied black students from Taliaferro access to the buses going to Warrenton and Greensboro, according to a story in the *Atlanta Constitution* on September 29, 1965.

Of the 139 white students from Taliaferro County, 24 were enrolled at Greene County High as part of Greene County's agreement with the federal government to comply with the Civil Rights Act of 1964.

The *Constitution* article includes mention that one of the reporters covering the story was Tom Brokaw of WSB television in Atlanta. Brokaw would go on to be one of the leading figures in the history of journalism.

According to the *Herald-Journal* of October 1, 1965, fifteen black students from Taliaferro County traveled to Greensboro seeking enrollment at Greene County High School after the August 27 deadline for admissions. According to the article, the students met with Principal Ellis Foster while two civil rights workers watched from across the street. Those students were not enrolled.

By November, the African American students from Taliaferro County who had been denied entrance in September were finally enrolled in the Warren County, Wilkes County, and Greene County schools.

In 1982, Greene and Taliaferro Counties merged their high schools to create Greene-Taliaferro High School in a new building located in Greensboro. But in 2001 Taliaferro County High School was reopened in Crawfordville. Today the Taliaferro County School System has 162 students in pre-K through twelfth grade.

FORD, BREEDING WORK TOGETHER

Trying to avoid the acrimony that had taken place in some of the surrounding counties, Greene County school superintendent Ford Boston, who was white, and Floyd T. Corry Elementary principal William J. Breeding, who was black, combined their considerable influence in hopes of keeping the temperature down on both sides.

"Daddy and Mr. Breeding were very tight," said Ford Boston's daughter, Elaine Boston Carsel. "They tried to keep everything calm. Daddy had the utmost respect for Mr. Breeding. They were the best two people you could have to handle a situation like that."

"My dad and Mr. Boston wanted a smooth transition," said Katrina Breeding. "I remember them talking on the phone all the time."

There was a plan. What remained to be seen was whether local leaders—both black and white—could execute the plan.

"At my house we were aware of what was going on," said Eric Ashley, whose parents, Billy and Mary Jean Ashley, were big supporters of the public schools. "There were people who didn't like [desegregation] and voiced it. But overall, our administrative people, black and white, had the courage to make this a smooth transition."

Thanks to the work of Boston, Breeding, and others, the groundwork had been laid for what everyone hoped would be a peaceful transition to full integration in the fall of 1970.

But there was one more mountain to climb before reaching that goal. And it would come in the fall of 1969.

3

THE KING AND QUEEN OF INTEGRATION

It was the summer of 1969, and Ellis Foster, the principal at predominately white Greene County High School, was playing golf with his friend Hughes Ash, a retired brigadier general of the United States Army.

Mr. Foster, a calm, steady man who loved the peace and quiet of the golf course, was distracted, and General Ash noticed it. Mr. Foster, it turned out, had a very important decision weighing on his mind.

Mr. Foster and Eli Jackson, his counterpart at predominately black Floyd T. Corry High School, had already met with Ford Boston, the white superintendent of the Greene County School System. With full integration set to come in the fall of 1970, and limited integration already taking place in some grades, the Greene County Board of Education had devised a plan for the 1969–1970 school year that would send buses of white juniors and seniors from Greene County High to Corry High to take English in the same classroom as African American students. As the board attempted to sell its plan for full integration in the 1970–1971 school year, it was important for an uncertain public to see that the road to integration would go both ways.

But Mr. Foster had a problem.

"I have to find two teachers who are willing to bus students over to Floyd T. Corry," he told General Ash.

Tommi Ward and Nicholas Antone, together again, with plaques they received for their work in the fall of 1969. Photo courtesy of Tommi Ward.

General Ash had a solution—or at least part of the solution.

His daughter, Tommi, had just come to live in Greene County while her husband, Rick, served in Vietnam. She was only twenty-one years old and had recently graduated from North Georgia College in Dahlonega, about ninety-five miles north of Greensboro.

"My daughter will do it," the general confidently told Mr. Foster.

"I grew up in the service going to integrated schools, so it wasn't a big deal to me," said Mrs. Ward.

"So he got me a job. He also got a job for my sister [whose husband was also in Vietnam], and we all moved to Greene County and went to work," said Mrs. Ward. "All [my dad] told me was, 'You're going to have to take your students to another school.'"

Mrs. Ward was paired with Margaret Eubanks, a veteran English teacher from Greene County High School. They worked with two African American teachers from Corry—Nicholas Antone and Barbara Christian.

Mr. Antone, a graduate of Alabama State College in Montgomery, liked the idea of smoothing the path to total integration with this experimental program.

"We met with Mr. Ford Boston, the superintendent, and he told us that this [integration] was going to happen, so that we should try to make this go as smoothly as possible," said Mr. Antone, who also served as a football coach at Corry.

There was a bit of uneasiness during some of the early classes.

"It was a nervous time for me," said Eric Ashley, our white offensive tackle. "I was aware of the meaning behind what we were doing. I wasn't convinced that this was the right way to do this, but I kept my feelings to myself. The thing that made it work was Tommi Ward and her humor. She kept things light."

On the first day in Mr. Antone's class, the black students sat on the far side of the room and remained there while the white students filed in and sat on the other side of the room.

"We had to fix that," said Mr. Antone, during an interview at his home in Greensboro. "I'd never assigned seats before, but we did the very next day, and it broke the ice.

"By the second day the students were talking to each other about hair and makeup and football and all that stuff that teenagers talk about. When the class was over, I had to get them to leave because they wanted to keep talking. The kids looked at each other and said, 'We'll see you tomorrow.' It was just a great feeling."

"Mr. Antone was just the best," said Elaine Boston Carsel. "He was a very special teacher."

The experiment of busing white students to Corry in the fall of 1969 served a dual purpose.

"After meeting the kids from Greene County, the students from Corry spread the word to the rest of their classmates that this had a chance to work," said Mr. Antone. "The kids from Greene County High told their friends that the students from Corry were just like everybody else. I think it really smoothed the way to what was going to happen the following year."

At the end of the 1969–1970 school year, Mrs. Ward, Mr.

Antone, Mrs. Christian, and Mrs. Eubanks were honored by the students at Floyd T. Corry.

The 1969–1970 yearbook at Greene County High School recognized the significance of busing white children to a predominately black school, and the role it would ultimately play in fully integrating the schools the following year:

> At the beginning of school an air of tension and a feeling of expectation accompanied the first trip to Corry High. Now students rush to the bus just as they would to any other class.

Today Mrs. Ward and Mr. Antone are still connected to each other, as they both serve on the adjunct faculty at Georgia Military College in Madison.

The fall of 2022 marked fifty-two years since they became the "king and queen" of integration at Greene County High School.

4

"THESE YOUNG MEN . . . ARE JUST LIKE YOU"

I'd like to tell you that when Greene County High School and Floyd T. Corry merged in the fall of 1970, the first thing I thought about was how historic the event was, both sociologically and politically.

But that wasn't the case. My first thought was about what kind of football team we were going to have once all the Corry guys came over.

First, some background.

Greene County High School, which had merged with Union Point High School in 1965, played in the Georgia High School Association (GHSA), which was the organizing body for athletics for the white schools across the state.

In 1969, the year before merging with Corry, Greene County was a member of GHSA Region 7-B. The football team finished third in the region with a 6–4 record after winning its last four games of the season. In Region 7-B, Greene County had some of its longest-standing rivals in Washington-Wilkes, Morgan County, Warren County, and Putnam County.

Floyd T. Corry, whose mascot was also the Tigers and who had the same school colors (gold and black), played in the Georgia Interscholastic Association (GIA), the organizing body for the black schools in the state. The GIA was founded in 1948 and held state championships until the end of the 1969–1970 academic year.

While Corry did not win any GIA state championships in football, the Corry girls' basketball team won state titles in 1959, 1960, and 1962 with William J. Breeding as coach.

As a GIA member, Corry played in District VI, Class A, along with other black schools in Eatonton, Gainesville, Madison, Warrenton, and Washington, just to name a few.

In 1966, the GHSA began inviting GIA schools to join and compete for championships. In 1970 the GIA closed operations.

C. S. VEAZEY BECOMES HEAD COACH

In 1962, Charlton S. Veazey, a Greensboro native who had left home at age sixteen to join the navy, returned to Greensboro and became the head football coach at Greensboro High School. Three years later Greensboro High merged with Union Point High to form Greene County High School. Union Point High did not have a football team, so it was natural that Coach Veazey became the first head football coach at Greene County High.

When Greene County and Floyd T. Corry merged in 1970, Coach Veazey was named head coach of the new football team. His top two assistant coaches would be Mack Poss, who had been at Greene County since 1967, and Larry Callair, one of four coaches who came over from Floyd T. Corry.

The other coaches from Corry were Nicholas Antone, Benny Asbury, and Nathaniel Whitehead. Dennis Fordham, who had been on the Greene County staff since 1968, was named assistant football coach and head boys' basketball coach.

It was a very strong staff.

"We didn't know it at the time, but we had a great group of coaches," said Tom Faust, a junior on the 1970 football team. "They were the perfect leaders to get us through what many believed was going to be a very difficult time."

I learned later that Coach Veazey made it clear to his staff

In the spring of 1970, Coach Veazey told his Greene County players, black and white, that there would be no conflict on the team. Photo courtesy of Greene County High School.

that it was up to them to keep the team together when times got tough. And they did get tough.

"Coach Veazey and the staff talked about it all the time," said Coach Poss. "This team was going to be together, and it was going to be unified. We were the new Greene County football team."

The structure of the football program at Corry had been different than that of Greene County, where Coach Veazey was clearly in charge.

"We really didn't have a head coach [at Corry] per se," said Charles Turner, who came from Corry to be the starting quarterback at the new Greene County in 1970. "We had one coach handling the offense and one handling the defense. We really didn't call them 'Coach.' We just called them 'Mister.'"

BOTH SCHOOLS HAD GOOD TALENT RETURNING

When Greensboro and Union Point merged to create Greene County High in 1965, a new football stadium was built at a cost of $50,000. Greene County played Washington-Wilkes in the first game in the new stadium, losing 40–8.

Corry played its games at Robinson Field (now Robinson Park), which was a brisk walk from Floyd T. Corry.

Prior to 1965, Greene County High School and Floyd T. Corry shared Robinson Field. If both were scheduled to be home on a particular weekend, then one school, usually Greene County, would play on Friday, and the other school would play on Saturday.

In the fall of 1969, the year before merging with Greene County, Floyd T. Corry's football team had a record of 4–5 with a squad of twenty-four players. But Corry had a lot of good players coming back for the fall of 1970, including Charles Turner at quarterback, running back Ben Allen Gresham, offensive tackle James Scott, linebacker Arthur Jackson, guard Guy Crutchfield, nose guard James Kimbro, and split end Mike Jackson.

Greene County had a bunch of skill players returning in running back/wide receiver Freddie Walker, one of the fastest guys in the state; running backs Al Cason and Tony Whittaker; and fullback/linebacker Dene Channell, who had been the team's starting quarterback the previous season.

HOW TWO TEAMS BECAME ONE

Given the quality of players returning from both schools, I expected us to have a good team when the schools merged.

But that was on paper. In the real world, it was clear to me that the new team had a lot of work to do.

There was an announcement in the *Herald-Journal* that spring practice for the new Greene County High School would start on May 1. On May 28, there would be a spring game at Tiger Stadium.

When spring practice was over and all heads were counted, our team had only nineteen players (twelve white, seven black).

I was really disappointed.

I thought there would be more players, especially since the two schools were merging to make a larger school. According to the Greene County High School 1970–1971 yearbook, nearly half of the 411 students in the sophomore, junior, and senior classes were male. How could we have only 19 guys who wanted to play football?

I talked to a lot of people about this question at the time but never got a satisfactory answer. Fifty years later, I still don't have an answer. I asked my teammates and coaches about it when I was doing the interviews for this book.

"I never understood why we had so few players," said Arthur Jackson. "I think some guys were scared. Football is hard. There is a lot of work involved."

"Yes, I was surprised that we only had nineteen players," said assistant coach Larry Callair. "We had several guys who dropped out. But the ones that were worth their salt did stay."

"WE WERE GOING TO BE THE BEST-CONDITIONED TEAM IN THE STATE"

As spring turned into summer, it became clear that, with so few players, this team was going to have to work extra hard just to be able to compete on a weekly basis.

"When the coaches met after spring practice, Coach Veazey made one thing very clear," said Coach Poss. "We were going to be the best-conditioned team in the state. A lot of guys were going to have to play both ways [offense and defense]. Other teams would try to wear us down. If we weren't in great shape, we wouldn't have a chance."

Coach Veazey expected—required, actually—something else from every man on our team, black or white: there would be, Coach Veazey said, absolutely *no* personal conflicts within the team. Some people were expecting us to fail, people who didn't believe that a racially integrated team could work together. He told us there were people who actually *hoped* we would fail.

This experiment in race relations was going to work because our head coach was demanding that it work.

On the first day of spring practice, the African American players were bused to Greene County High from Corry. Before they arrived, Coach Veazey gathered his Greene County players together. He made it crystal clear what he expected from us in terms of behavior.

"These young men coming from Corry are just like you," he said. "They want to play football and they want to win. They have families who care about them and support them. They are your teammates."

During the interview process for this book, I asked all the players about this, and they could remember only one skirmish in practice between a black player and a white player.

"Edward Stapleton and Guy Crutchfield locked horns during practice one day," said Dene Channell. "It didn't last very long."

"Yeah, Edward and I got after it a little bit. He was a tough dude. But after it was over, we were fine. He was a really good football player," said Guy. "It's football. I'm glad he was on my side."

"What I remember is that the guys got along pretty much all the time," said Dene. "We knew that people were watching us."

We would have loose ball drills where one of the coaches would throw a football on the ground and you and one other player would basically have to outfight the other guys for possession. I remember Charles Turner getting into a scrap with Eric Ashley (who was white) during a loose ball drill. But the hard feelings never lasted long.

"That was pretty wild," said Charles, with a laugh.

NO DOUBT: CHARLES TURNER WAS THE STARTING QB

A lot of questions needed to be answered in the spring of 1970. But the identity of our starting quarterback was not one of them.

I've covered college football for forty-six years, and in that time, I have seen a number of players who had what I call the

"IT" factor. This quality is hard to describe. It is simply a presence that exudes confidence and the ability to back up that confidence on the field.

I knew from the first time I met him and shook his hand in the spring of 1970 that Charles Turner had "IT." The other players—both black and white—knew it too.

"The day that Charles Turner got off the bus it was clear to everybody that he was going to be our starting quarterback," said Tommy Moon, who is white, and who would start at center for most of the 1970 season. "He's one of the best athletes I've ever seen."

Dene Channell, who is white, had been the starting quarterback at Greene County High School the year before.

"I was perfectly fine with the decision" to make Charles Turner the starting quarterback, said Dene. "Charles was a great athlete and he could help us win. Besides, I told the coaches I wanted to play fullback and linebacker so that I could hit people on every play."

Before the two schools merged, Charles had told the coaches at Corry that he really wanted to play wide receiver his senior year because he loved running routes and catching the ball. As a junior at Corry in the 1969 season, he caught four touchdown passes in a single game. And wide receiver, he thought, was probably going to be his position if he played college football.

But the coaches convinced Charles that our team needed him at quarterback. With his immense athletic ability, he gave our team its best chance to win.

And I learned of another factor in this decision in the process of doing research for this book.

Given all the change that was about to happen in the fall of 1970, it was very important to the African American community in Greene County that Charles be the team's starting quarterback. That message, said Charles, was delivered loud and clear.

"I had been brought up to respect my elders and the leaders of our community," said Charles. "This is what they expected me to do."

Charles's mother, Chloe, was a lifelong educator, and his father, Charlie, owned his own business and was one of the most respected people in his community. Charles knew exactly what was expected of him and his sister, Janice.

He was the unquestioned leader of the African American students who had to say goodbye to Floyd T. Corry and enroll at Greene County High School in the fall of 1970. He accepted his role.

LOSING TO THE SENIORS IN THE SPRING GAME

Because our team had only nineteen players, there were not enough bodies to have a traditional spring game. So it was decided that the outgoing seniors from Corry and Greene County would combine to field a team and play the varsity.

Coach Veazey asked Coach Antone to handle the outgoing seniors for the spring game.

"It was an interesting atmosphere," said Coach Antone of the spring game. "A lot of folks were cheering for our new team, but a lot of folks were also pulling for the seniors."

We got ahead early in the game, but then Coach Antone unleashed his best weapon—a big, powerful running back from Corry named Andrew Barrow. And once Barrow got rolling, we didn't have anybody who could get him on the ground. The exception to that rule was Ben Allen Gresham, a smallish running back/defensive back, who could get low enough to tackle Barrow.

But Barrow and the other seniors were too much for us. We lost the game.

It was only a spring game. It really didn't mean anything. But that's not how it felt. I was really mad. Charles Turner was even madder.

"I wasn't a very good sport back in those days. There is no way we should have lost to the seniors," he said.

"But in the long run losing that spring game was probably good for us. It made us realize that if we were going to win, we would have to step it up. With only nineteen guys, nobody was going to give us anything. We knew right then that we were going to have to work very, very hard if we wanted to compete in the fall."

By the end of spring practice, the 19 of Greene had already bonded. After only a month together, we were a TEAM.

"You could feel it. The guys were coming together," said Arthur Jackson. "The other players I talked to couldn't wait to get through the summer and get back to work."

But what about the new Greene County High School and its newly integrated student body? Would it bond? What was going to happen with full integration of the students, the faculty, and the athletic teams?

Those of us on the football team got along because we had something very important in common—wanting to win football games. We were willing to work together to achieve that goal.

By the time school started back in the fall of 1970, the 19 of Greene had worked together for a month in the spring and for several more weeks in the heat of August. We had had a crash course on learning how to get along.

The other students at Greene County did not have that opportunity—at least not to the extent that those of us on the football team did. How would full integration play out within the student body as a whole? We were about to find out.

"I'll admit it. I was a little apprehensive when school began," said Eric Ashley. "We thought it was going to be okay. But we didn't know. We really didn't know what to expect."

"I felt good about our football team because you could tell the guys were all getting along," said Charles Turner. "I hoped the same thing would be true when we started school. But I didn't know how it was going to go. None of us did."

5

"IT WAS NOT ALL SWEETNESS AND LIGHT"

In the fall of 1970, Greene County did not face a lot of the organized resistance to integration that nearby counties such as Taliaferro and Hancock were experiencing.

Taliaferro, whose county seat was Crawfordville, closed its
all-white school—Alexander Stephens Institute—rather than
integrate. Public demonstrations brought out the Georgia State
Patrol to restore order. The turmoil got to the point where the
Atlanta television stations made the two-hour trip to Taliaferro
to cover it.

The Ku Klux Klan held a march in Sparta—the seat of Hancock County—to protest the integration of Sparta High School
and Hancock Central High.

Sure, there was tension in Greene County, particularly in the
early days of the school year. I thought this tension was based on
the fact that we simply didn't know what outside forces might
come into play.

"I remember some protesters coming from out of town trying
to make trouble," said Dene Channell, whose father was on the
Greene County school board. "But they didn't stay long because
nothing was happening. Nothing was going to happen. That is
not what the people of Greene County wanted. We wanted to
make this [integration] work."

I believe that the incremental approach that Greene County

took in the years leading up to complete integration served as a pressure relief valve when full integration finally arrived.

"We already had some African American students at Greene County who chose to come early," Dene said. "Then we made the decision to bus students over to Corry to take English in my junior year [1969–1970]. Those things got everybody used to the idea of going to school with people of another race. It happened gradually instead of all at once."

Another factor in the relative calm in Greene County was sensitivity among the faculty that the students from Corry had given up quite a lot to make this work for all students—black and white. Floyd T. Corry had a rich tradition, and its students had to walk away from that.

"We all wanted to graduate from Corry," said Fannie Peaks, a black senior in the 1970–1971 graduating class at Greene County. "I have to admit that we did not want to come [to Greene County]. But they said, 'No, you have to go here.' Things were very different, but I thought we adjusted very quickly."

Fannie and several other black classmates said the transition was easier than they thought it would be.

"I first thought they [white students] were going to run all over us when we got there," Fannie continued. "We thought we were going to get a lot of pushback, but it wasn't like that at all. So we had to adjust to that, because we had the mentality of 'they didn't want us over there.'"

"The boys were actually more cordial than the girls. We just kept at them until they finally accepted us."

I have tried to imagine what it would have felt like had I been told I had to leave Greene County High School for my senior year and go to another school where I might not be accepted. I've concluded that the black students I met and got to know my senior year handled the transition a lot better than I would have.

In October 2022, I did a final series of interviews for this book in which I specifically asked my African American classmates if they had experienced any overt racism from white students in the fall of 1970.

"I know people find it hard to believe, but things really went smoothly," said Ben Allen Gresham, a junior from Corry. "I was treated with respect by all the white students. There really wasn't a problem."

When it came time to name the "Senior Superlatives" for the 1970–1971 yearbook, the decision was made that each category—Most Athletic, Most Dependable, and so on—would be represented by both a white couple and a black couple.

A pair of white students—Edward Stapleton and Meme Morgan—were named Mr. and Miss Senior. A pair of black students—Charles Turner and Celeste Booker—were Mr. and Miss Greene County High School.

Two black students—Arthur Jackson and Mary Williams—joined two white students—Al Cason and Meme Morgan—as Most Athletic.

And so on. I thought it was a good way to recognize the contributions from both schools to the new Greene County High School.

"It just seemed like the right thing to do," said Tommi Ward, a faculty advisor for the yearbook. "We ran it past Mr. Foster and Mr. Jackson [the principal and associate principal], and they signed off on it."

Not everyone agreed.

"I just didn't like that," said Earnest Edmondson, a black student and member of the band. "You honor the students who have earned the award. I just don't think it should have been handled that way."

Just because things went relatively smoothly at Greene County High School when compared to surrounding counties doesn't mean there were NO problems.

Ground zero at GCHS was the principal's office, where the steady Ellis Foster tried to keep things on an even keel.

Mr. Foster had been in the Greene County School System as a coach, teacher, and administrator since 1949. He had been chosen by Ford Boston, the superintendent of the Greene County

Charles Turner and Celeste Booker were Mr. and Miss GCHS. Photo courtesy of Greene County High School.

School System, for the challenge of leading the combined schools through a historic transition.

Eli Jackson, the beloved principal at Floyd T. Corry High, was named associate principal at Greene County High.

Because of his long tenure in the Greene County School System and his calm, supportive demeanor, the faculty was very loyal to Mr. Foster.

"My mother and Mr. Foster were very close," said Eric Ashley, a senior offensive tackle. "They spent a lot of time talking about various situations that occurred at school. He knew he could bounce stuff off of her."

Mr. Foster died in 2008, but I talked to his daughter, Kathie, who was a junior at Greene County High during the 1970–1971 school year.

"If Daddy had any fears or major concerns about what was going to happen [that fall], he never shared them with us," said Kathie, who now lives in Hartwell, Georgia. "I just know that he was concerned about things going smoothly."

Christine West, Mr. Foster's longtime administrative assistant, had high praise for his leadership skills and equanimity under fire.

"Mr. Foster was steady. He was a very good leader," said Mrs. West.

But the reality, said Mrs. West when I sat with her, was that "not everything was as calm and smooth as people liked to believe it was."

There were two major incidents that were unnerving to me and my classmates—black and white.

I will never forget the fight in the main parking lot between Keiter Parrott, a black student, and Bodie Vandiver, a white student, that resulted in Vandiver being stabbed.

Coach Poss and Coach Callair had to sprint to separate the two students and drag them back into the school. There was a lot of blood, and a lot of uneasy, scared feelings throughout the school that lasted for a few days.

My black teammate Ben Allen Gresham and I watched the episode unfold as we stood near the back door of the school that led to the main parking lot.

"This is bad, Ben. Really bad," I told him.

"Yeah," he said. "I was hoping that this was not going to happen."

When I sat down with Ben Allen to discuss this book, he said the memory of that day was still strong.

"I will never forget it," he said.

Three years later, on December 2, 1973, the *Herald-Journal* reported that Keiter Parrott had shot and killed Bodie Vandiver. According to court documents, Parrott served almost ten years in prison and was paroled in 1984.

Another serious incident occurred when a student, Tony Shelton, was caught smoking in the boys' restroom by Coach Dennis Fordham. Coach Fordham escorted Shelton to Mr. Foster's office.

"I was a third-year teacher who thought it was my job to police the world," said Coach Fordham when we met in his home in Covington, Georgia. "I took it upon myself to check in the bathroom between classes."

Coach Fordham said that by the time he and Shelton reached Mr. Foster's office, the conversation between them was getting pretty heated.

The door to Mr. Foster's office door contained a sheet of glass with safety wire built in to prevent it from shattering. Shelton and Coach Fordham were exchanging words when Shelton exploded and put his hand through the glass, severely injuring himself. Mr. Foster told Coach Fordham to leave his office, and medical people were called.

"It was very scary," said Mrs. West.

"We understood that things were not going to be perfect," said Charles Turner. "But our job as football players and students was to stay away from that kind of stuff."

"It was not all sweetness and light," said Tom Faust. "If we had any issues on the team we worked them out. There were problems [elsewhere in the school], but we didn't allow those things to intrude on the cocoon of the football team."

At the end of the school year, Mr. Foster left Greene County High School to become principal at Hart County Junior High in Hartwell, Georgia.

"Mr. Foster decided it was time to move on to the next chapter," said Mrs. West.

Mrs. West also moved on, becoming an administrative assistant at Nathanael Greene Academy. Today she is an administrative assistant at the First Baptist Church in Greensboro.

The following school year (1971–1972), Evans Acree took over as principal of Greene County High School.

Eli Jackson, who had given a lifetime of service to educating the children of Greene County, retired.

6

FROM 0–2 TO DIVISION CHAMPS

When Greene County High School merged with Floyd T. Corry High, it became a new and larger school.

As a result, in athletics, Greene County moved from Region 7-B to Region 8-AA, where our football team would play bigger schools, mostly to the north of us. And we were going to face these tougher teams with only nineteen players.

"It didn't take us long to figure out we were going to play a higher level of competition," said Coach Mack Poss. "But we looked at the players we had and thought we were going to be just fine."

Our start to the 1970 season was anything *but* fine, as we lost our first two games—both nonregion—to Putnam County and Warren County.

"That wasn't what we expected," said Charles Turner. "But we still thought we were going to be okay. We just knew our team was going to take some time to jell. We had to remember that this group of guys had never played together."

After that 0–2 start, we won seven of our last eight regular-season games to capture the East Division championship of Region 8-AA, Greene County's first football championship since 1956. Greene County would go on to play West Division champion Gainesville High School for the region title.

"By the end of the year I thought we had a really good team," said running back Tony Whittaker. "I thought we could beat just about anybody."

GOING TO AL CASON'S HOUSE

On a cold, rainy day in January 2020, I drove to Milledgeville, Georgia, to have lunch with Al Cason, our outstanding running back. Al was a pharmacist at Central State Hospital in Milledgeville for thirty-four years and now lives in a beautiful home tucked quietly into some one hundred acres between Milledgeville and Sandersville.

Drawing on various sources, Al and Dene Channell were able to put together a DVD of all eleven games Greene County High School played in the fall of 1970. And on that unforgettable afternoon, Al and I watched every play of all eleven games.

He provided a running commentary from his steel trap of a memory. I took notes.

Whenever he got the ball in the game we were watching, Al would yell, "Run, Albert!!!!!" Whenever I missed a block, which happened frequently, Al would give me a hard time. He gave me a hard time because, more often than not, the guy I failed to block ended up tackling him.

We had an absolute blast.

The following game summaries come from reports in the *Herald-Journal*, from watching the videos, and from notes gleaned from the interviews I did with the players and coaches about the games.

1970 GREENE COUNTY TIGERS
RECORD: 7–4

> *Game 1: Putnam County 14, Greene County 6*
> *August 28, 1970, in Eatonton, Georgia*

This game was originally scheduled to be played later in the season, but a conflict moved it to the last Friday in August.

This was a nonconference game against one of our longtime rivals from Greene County's previous conference affiliation. We knew the final score was going to be close because it was always a tough game when we played these guys.

Putnam County still had not forgiven Greene County for spoiling its perfect season three years earlier. In 1967 the Blue Devils—led by an incredible running back named Brent Cunningham, who went on to start for three seasons at Georgia Tech—came to Tiger Stadium with a 7–0 record and the No. 1 ranking in the state. That season Putnam County beat every team on its schedule by twelve points or more.

Except one.

Greene County and Putnam County were tied 26–26 in the final minutes of that 1967 game because Putnam County had lost its kicker, Bill Haley, to an injury and the Blue Devils had missed a couple of extra points. When Putnam County got the ball back for its last possession, their coach, Al Reaves, put Cunningham back in the shotgun formation and just let him run it on every play.

"Coach Reaves had gotten the idea from another coach, and Brent was so good it really worked," said Charles Winslette, a player on that 1967 Putnam County team who later became the head coach at Greene County, winning a state championship in 1993. "I thought we were going to score and win the game."

As the final seconds ticked off the clock, Cunningham raced around his left end and appeared to have a clear path to the end zone. But just before Cunningham reached the goal line, the Greene County safety, Tommy Turner, dove and knocked him out of bounds at the one-yard line.

Time ran out.

The scoreboard said 26–26.

But Greene County won the game.

Putnam County won its next four games that year by a combined score of 150–20 and captured a state championship. The Blue Devils finished 11–0–1. That Greene County team finished 3–6–1.

In the game with Putnam County in 1970, Charles Turner threw a touchdown pass to Al Cason just a few minutes into the second quarter to give us a 6–0 lead. But as the game wore on, I could tell that our lack of depth was beginning to show. Putnam County scored on a sixteen-yard run by Larry Dunn in the third quarter, and then Russell Haley, brother of Bill, ran sixty-nine yards for a score. Greene County had only ninety-nine total yards. Putnam County was 6–4 that season.

Game 2: Warren County 10, Greene County 0
September 4, 1970, in Warrenton, Georgia

The energy level in our locker room was always a little higher whenever we played Warren County. That's because Warren County was coached by Hale Burnette, a former player for Coach Veazey at Greensboro High School before it merged with Union Point High.

This would be Coach Veazey's fourth meeting with Coach Burnette, who took over as head coach at Warren County in 1967 and won a state championship in 1968. Coach Veazey was 0–3 against him.

"Coach Veazey always had a little more pep in his step when we were getting ready to play Warren County," Coach Poss said. "He did not like losing to Coach Burnette."

But we were really beat up after the first game with Putnam County. Al Cason and Tony Whittaker, two of our best running backs, did not play due to injuries.

The game was also played in a driving rain.

As it turned out, this was one of Hale Burnette's best teams ever, as the Warren County Blue Devils went 12–0 before losing to Roswell in the Class A state championship game.

Game 3: Greene County 28, Georgia Military College 12
September 11, 1970, in Milledgeville, Georgia

This was Greene County's third consecutive road game, and man, did we need a win—any kind of a win.

Georgia Military College was a service-based institution that offered junior college, high school, and middle school academic programs. GMC was Class B, and Greene County was Class AA. This was absolutely a game we should win, and win comfortably.

"Nobody wanted to be 0–3. We knew we were going to have to step things up a little bit," said Arthur Jackson.

The visitor's dressing area at GMC was pretty sparse. But it was near the GMC pool, and Coach Veazey promised that if we won the game, he'd let us swim in the pool for a while before we headed home to Greensboro.

The field was wet and sloppy, and we just couldn't get our offense going early.

The score was tied at 6–6 at the end of the first half. When Coach Veazey walked into the dressing room, I thought he was going to be furious. Instead, he went up to the blackboard and calmly started drawing a couple of plays.

"Listen to me and you'll win this game," he said.

I heard him loud and clear.

And we did win.

The big play of the night was Freddie Walker's long punt return for a touchdown, which gave us a 19–6 lead. The sloppy turf did not slow him down one bit.

"Freddie looked like a great racehorse on a wet track running back that punt," center Tommy Moon said. "There was no way those guys from GMC were going to catch him."

Ben Allen Gresham tacked on a late touchdown, and we had our first win of the season.

And then the Tigers went swimming.

I remember that Coach Veazey wouldn't let anybody go in the deep end.

We had to get everybody home safely to get ready for our first home game of the year. I remember the players wondering out loud what kind of reception our team would get. I sure was glad we had beaten GMC.

Game 4: Greene County 7, Franklin County 6
September 18, 1970, in Greensboro

After three straight games on the road, it was good to finally be home.

Franklin County High School was located in Carnesville, about sixty-five miles north of Greensboro. This was the first time Greene County had ever played Franklin County in the sport of football.

It became clear early on that it was going to be a defensive battle.

The score was 0–0 at halftime.

In the third quarter, Freddie Walker returned a punt fifty-five yards for a touchdown. It was Freddie's second straight game with a punt return for a score. Eric Ashley made what would prove to be a crucial extra point to put us up 7–0.

Al Cason seemingly scored on a fifty-five-yard run that would have put the game away, but the referees called the play back on an illegal procedure penalty, which Al said was on me while we were watching the DVD together. I suggested that the video was "inconclusive."

Then we almost gave the game away. Franklin County's Mike Randall picked up the ball on a blocked punt in the final minutes of the game and ran thirty yards for a touchdown. Franklin County, sensing it had the momentum, went for the two-point conversion and the win. The play was stopped inches short of the goal line, and we won 7–6.

We had three pass interceptions in the game.

"The game shouldn't have been that close," said Ben Allen Gresham, our running back. "We had a much better team than they did, but we didn't put them away when we had the chance."

Ben Allen was right. Lesson learned. And we learned it without losing.

According to the *Herald-Journal*, Greene County had only sixteen players dressed for this game due to injuries.

Game 5: Monroe Area 24, Greene County 21
September 24, 1970, in Greensboro

I believe Monroe Area was the best team we played during the regular season.

"We had seen some of their guys during track season the previous spring," said Coach Poss. "They could flat run."

We appeared to have the game under control, leading at halftime 21–12. But in the second half we began to wear down because of our lack of depth. We were still playing only about sixteen guys.

Another factor was that in the days leading up to the Monroe game, the seniors convinced Coach Veazey to let us change the sports drink we used during games. We had been drinking some nasty green stuff called Take Five. The new drink tasted so much better. But it didn't work. In the third quarter guys started cramping up.

Monroe scored twelve points in the fourth quarter, including the winning touchdown in the final minute.

"We had them," said Charles Turner. "We just let that game get away. No excuse for that."

"Of all the games we lost, that one made me the maddest," said Eric Ashley. "There is absolutely no way we should have lost that game."

So now we were 2–3 with an open date coming up.

It was crunch time. There were five games left in the regular season. Another loss and we were likely out of the running to win the East Division of Region 8-AA.

Everybody on our team—all nineteen of us—knew what we had to do.

"We didn't have a choice," said Charles Turner. "We had to win the rest of them."

Game 6: Greene County 22, Stephens County 6
October 9, 1970, in Greensboro

The winner of this game would lead the East Division of Region 8-AA. Greene County had not won any sort of football championship since 1956.

Al Cason scored the first touchdown of the night on an eleven-yard run. Charles Turner then threw to Dene Channell for a two-point conversion to give Greene County an 8–0 lead.

We scored again with twenty-nine seconds left in the first half when Charles threw a fifty-two-yard pass to Freddie Walker. It was a beautiful throw, and a beautiful catch by Freddie, who had gotten behind the Stephens County secondary. Greene County led 15–0 at halftime.

Neither team scored in the third quarter. In the fourth quarter Charles scored on an eight-yard run to make it 22–0 with nine minutes left. Stephens County didn't score their touchdown until late in the game.

Greene County was 3–3 with four games left. The good news was that three of those four games would be at home.

Game 7: Greene County 21, Hart County 0
October 16, 1970, in Hartwell, Georgia

After three straight home games, we went back on the road. It would be the last time we would play away from Tiger Stadium during the regular season.

It was homecoming at Hart County High School, but we were in no mood to let them celebrate. I felt like this was a big test. We needed to take care of business and head back to Greene County for our last three games.

Hart County was 0–6 and had nothing to lose. We had the better team and had everything to lose. Those kinds of games always scare me.

But we had no reason to be scared on this night. We ran for 280 yards, and Hart County couldn't do anything to stop us. Al Cason scored two touchdowns, and Tony Whittaker had one.

Edward Stapleton blocked a punt, which set up a touchdown.

Game 8: Greene County 13, Lincoln County 6
October 23, 1970, in Greensboro

Lincoln County was a nonregion opponent, which meant we could lose this game and still go to the region championship.

But this was a very important game for us because of Coach Poss.

Coach Poss grew up in Lincolnton, the county seat of Lincoln County. Since coming to Greene County in 1967, he was 3–0 against his old school.

"Yep, the game meant a lot to me," said Coach Poss. "It's home, and you don't want to go home after losing to them."

By this point, the Greene County community was really starting to rally behind our football team.

"People were excited because we were winning and we had a really good group of guys who cared about each other," said Dene Channell. "They knew we had a chance to do something special."

Lincoln County had an all-state player at quarterback in Alvin Scott, but it wouldn't be enough for the Red Devils to hang with us on this night.

According to the *Herald-Journal*, there was a standing-room-only crowd at Tiger Stadium, and they got their money's worth.

Greene County opened the game with a bang, as the Tigers defense threw Lincoln County's offense for a loss on each of its first three plays.

"Our crowd gave us a standing ovation," said Al Cason. "I will never forget that."

Al returned a punt sixty-five yards for a touchdown. That made it 7–0 until Lincoln County blocked a punt and recovered it on the Greene County four-yard line. They scored three plays later, but a two-point conversion try was no good, and Greene County held on to a 7–6 lead.

Late in the game, Tommy Moon, our center, fell on the ball in the end zone when one of our backs fumbled going in for a touchdown. That score and an extra point gave us the final margin.

We played our best defensive game of the season, holding Lincoln County to only two first downs.

So now we were 5–3 overall, and 3–0 in the East Division of Region 8-AA. We had division games left with Madison County and Morgan County. Winning those games would give Greene County the division championship. Both games would be at home.

Game 9: Greene County 30, Madison County 6
October 30, 1970, in Greensboro

In a school year filled with firsts, here was another. This game marked Greene County's first homecoming celebration as a fully integrated school.

Willie Belle Miller became the first African American to be named homecoming queen of the new Greene County High School.

The game was never in doubt, as we dominated Madison County (1–7) with 292 yards rushing.

Al Cason scored two early touchdowns, on a three-yard run and a twenty-seven-yard pass from Charles Turner. Charles also had a twenty-yard run for a touchdown. We led 18–6 at halftime.

But the thing Charles remembers most about the game was seeing a cute cheerleader from Madison County named Cynthia Freeman. He didn't meet her until later in the school year when Vera Cochran, a Greene County cheerleader, introduced them at a basketball game at Madison County.

They started dating after Charles's sophomore year in college. They have been married for forty-seven years.

In the second half, Tony Whittaker scored on a one-yard run, and Ben Allen Gresham scored on a three-yard run.

Now we had a week off before playing our big rival, Morgan County, for the East Division championship. That game would also be the last home game for our seniors.

Game 10: Greene County 28, Morgan County 6
November 13, 1970, in Greensboro

A photo of Greene County's nine seniors—James Scott (74), Arthur Jackson (32), Al Cason (22), Charles Turner (11), Tony Barnhart (50), Eric Ashley (73), Dene Channell (12), Edward Stapleton (82), and Freddie Walker (20)—made the front page of the *Herald-Journal* before the game.

It was a historic photo, because it showed black and white players together representing the senior class at Greene County High School and what would have been the senior class at Floyd T. Corry for the first time.

Morgan County and Greene County have been rivals since 1917. Proximity has something to do with that, as the county seats of Madison and Greensboro are about twenty minutes apart.

This would turn out to be one of the biggest games the two schools had ever played against each other, because the winner would capture the East Division of Region 8-AA and play Gainesville a week later for the region championship.

A story in the *Herald-Journal* said that it was the largest crowd of the season at Tiger Stadium. The nineteen members of our team had all come so far since the previous spring, when the team was first being put together. Now Greene County was one victory away from having the opportunity to play for a region championship.

By this time, Charles Turner and I had become close friends. On the Thursday before this crucial game, I asked him how he felt.

"There is no way we're going to lose this game," he said.

Greene County scored the first time it had the ball, driving fifty yards in seven plays. Al Cason scored from three yards out.

In the second quarter, Ben Allen Gresham picked up a Morgan County fumble and ran it in from twenty yards out to make it 14–0.

Tigers play Morgan County, Here Friday Night For 8-AA East Crown

NINE SENIORS PLAY LAST HOME GAME

Nine Greene County seniors would play their last home game against Morgan County on November 13, 1970. Photo courtesy of the *Herald-Journal*.

In the third quarter, we put together one of our best drives of the season, moving the ball eighty yards in fourteen plays. The drive lasted nine minutes and ended with a six-yard touchdown run to make it 21–0.

When the game was over, the players carried Coach Veazey to midfield on their shoulders. It was Greene County's first football championship since 1956, and Coach Veazey's first championship ever.

What made it special was that two schools and two communities had combined their talents and bonded in pursuit of a goal that everyone could be proud of.

A team whose journey had begun with so much uncertainty the previous spring had earned the right to continue playing football into the cool of November. The 19 of Greene still had at least one more game to play.

Tigers Win 8-AA East Title, Play Gainesville High There Friday For 8-AA Region Crown

8-AA EAST CHAMPIONS

Front row, left to right: 10, Tommy Moon; 11, Charles Turner; 12, Dene Channell; 20, Freddie Walker; 21, David Barnhart; 30, Al Cason; 32, Arthur Jackson. Middle row: 40, Tony Whittaker; 41, Ben Gresham; 42, Ricky Easley; 50, Tony Barnhart; 62, Guy Crutchfield; 64, Charles Martin; 70, James Kimbro. Back row: Coach Larry Callair, 73; Eric Ashley, 74; James Scott, 80; Mike Jackson, 81; Tommy Faust, 82; Edward Stapleton. Coach Mack Poss, Head Coach C. S. Veazey.

Greene County beat Morgan County to set up the big game with Gainesville for the Region 8-AA championship. Photo courtesy of the *Herald-Journal*.

A BIGGER TEAM . . . BUT NOT A BIGGER HEART

Gainesville 13, Greene County 0
November 20, 1970, in Gainesville, Georgia

It is seventy-eight miles from Greensboro to Gainesville, Georgia.

But in so many ways we felt like we were going to the moon when we traveled to the seat of Hall County to play Gainesville High School for the Region 8-AA championship.

Gainesville was one of the great high school football powers in the state of Georgia. The Red Elephants were coached by future Hall of Famer Bobby Gruhn, who won 254 games and sixteen region championships in his thirty years as a coach. The field at City Park, where we would play that night, bears his name today.

During the regular season, we rode a school bus to road games. But on this day, for this historic game, we went first class, riding a chartered Greyhound bus to Gainesville. We had made the "big time."

"That was impressive," Charles Turner said. "Very, very impressive."

It was a cold, damp night when the Greyhound bus pulled into City Park.

It had been raining hard all week, and there were even discussions, we were told, about moving the game to a later date or a different location.

That was not going to happen.

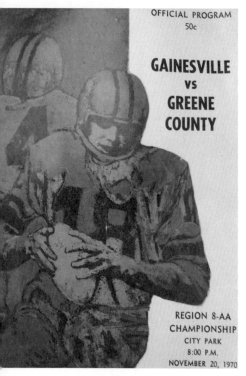

OFFICIAL PROGRAM
50c

GAINESVILLE
VS
GREENE
COUNTY

REGION 8-AA
CHAMPIONSHIP
CITY PARK
8:00 P.M.
NOVEMBER 20, 1970

It's the real t

GAINESVILLE HIGH SCHOOL

No.	Name	Po.	Cl.	Wt.	No.	Name	Po.	Cl.	Wt.
10	Jerry Kinsey	QB	11	182	60	Jimmy Jones	OG	12	171
11	David Perron	DHB	12	140	61	Johnny Yarbrough	DE	12	170
12	Tommy West	HB	11	192	62	Louis Adams	OT	11	175
13	David Brinson	DHB	10	140	64	Micky Neidenbach	LB	12	165
14	Nat Strong	DHB	11	140	65	Stanley Hall	G	10	140
16	Leland Byrd	QB	10	125	65	Chet Dukes	LB	10	160
17	Trece Battle	K	11	145	66	Mitchell Burnes	OG	12	185
18	Terry Wright	QB	10	141	67	David Murphy	OG	12	164
20	Reggie Sexton	TB	12	175	68	Tony Underwood	OG	10	185
21	Terry Phillips	HB	12	145	71	Phil Mathis	DT	12	205
23	Bobby Wright	TB	9	142	71	Larry Merritt	DT	11	220
25	Al Milne	DHB	11	150	72	David Jared	OT	12	170
26	Joe Ingram	TB	12	160	73	Buddy Henry	OT	10	190
27	Dwight Ellenburg	DHB	11	120	74	Ricky Stargel	DT	10	170
30	Lloyd Wherry	DHB	11	170	75	Eddie Lipscomb	DE	12	180
31	Walter Durden	LB	10	145	76	R. Pendergrass	OT	11	180
32	Miller Deaton	FB	12	200	77	Stan Cox	OT	10	166
35	Rick Snider	FB	11	145	78	David Ginn	T	10	140
39	Sidney Gardner	DHB	10	140	78	Rex Greene	OT	12	170
40	Bruce Burch (C)	DHB	12	160	79	Tony Bennett	DT	12	210
41	Calvin Young	HB	10	145	80	Mike Robertson	TE	12	196
42	Charles Young	HB	11	140	81	Chip Reed	TE	12	150
44	Jim Grogan	FB	10	150	81	David Stribling	SE	10	140
45	Chuck Walls	LB	10	150	82	Jimmy Smith	SE	11	173
46	Billy Jacobs	FB	10	145	83	Wes Phillips	TE	10	140
50	Bruce Roper	OG	10	170	84	Roger Dyer	TE	11	185
51	Tommy Phillips	C	12	220	85	Lin Zoller	DE	11	155
52	Frank Strickland	DG	10	177	85	David Dye	SE	12	165
53	Greg Mathis	M	10	146	86	Heyward Hosch	DE	11	175
54	John Garth	C	12	180	86	Mike Murray	DE	10	161
55	Jay Wright (C)	LB	12	170	88	Ronnie Soles	TE	12	150
57	Dick Valentine	C	10	150	89	David Boulware	DHB	12	150
58	Steve Wilson	OG	10	155					

COACHES		MANAGERS	
Bobby Gruhn	Chuck McDonald	Ricky Phillips	Tony Black
Andy Turk	Durward Pennington	Edward Hunter	Wayne Simmons
Bob Alexander	Jim Presnell	Andy Fuller	Bobby Howell

The front of the official program for the Region 8-AA championship game between Gainesville and Greene County on November 20, 1970. Photo courtesy of Al Cason.

Gainesville dressed out sixty-five players for the region championship game. Photo courtesy of Al Cason.

Our strength was speed and quickness. There was no way they would move the game and give us a shot at Gainesville on a dry surface.

"For us to be in a region championship game was something totally foreign to [Greene County High School]," said Eric Ashley. "I just remember how soggy that field was. It was like we were playing in a pigsty."

There was no getting around it: this was a classic David versus Goliath game. Greene County was playing one of the state's powerhouse football programs. The Red Elephants were 9–1, with

GREENE COUNTY HIGH SCHOOL

No.	Name	Po.	Cl.	Wt.
10	Tommy Moon	B	10	160
11	Charles Turner	B	12	165
12	Dene Channell	B	12	170
20	Freddie Walker	B	12	160
21	David Barnhart	B	10	155
22	Al Cason	B	12	170
32	Arthur Jackson	B	12	170
40	Tony Whittaker	B	11	160
41	Ben Gresham	B	11	140
50	Tony Barnhart	C	12	175
62	Guy Crutchfield	G	11	200
64	Charles Martin	G	10	150
70	James Kimbro	T	10	170
73	Eric Ashley	T	12	185
74	James Scott	T	12	230
80	Mike Jackson	E	11	155
82	Edward Stapleton	E	12	170
81	Tommy Faust	E	11	150

HEAD COACH—C. S. Veazey, University of Georgia

ASST. COACH—Mack Poss, Georgia Southern

ASST. COACH—Larry Callair, South Carolina State

ASST. COACHES—Dennis Fordham, Nicholas Antone, Nathan Whitehead, Bennie Asbury

MANAGERS—Dennis Mize, Charlie Veazey, Byron Cosby

TRAINER—Stan Jackson

BAND DIRECTOR—Joe V. Walters

Greene County dressed out only eighteen players for the game against Gainesville. Photo courtesy of Al Cason.

Gainesville Edges Greene County Tigers 13-0, In Class AA State Football Play-Off

Gainesville beats Greene County 13–0 for the Region 8-AA championship. It was the last game the 19 of Greene would play together. Photo courtesy of the *Herald-Journal*.

their only regular-season loss coming to St. Pius X of Atlanta by a score of 16–7.

And we were playing on their field. Their damned slick, treacherous, muddy field.

"All week long we kept talking about how big and strong and deep they were," said Coach Poss. "That was what we said in public."

But inside our locker room, the conversations about Gainesville were much different.

"The coaches kept telling us all week that we could beat those guys," said Arthur Jackson. "But they also told us it would be a tough game and that they would try to wear us down. Everybody had to be prepared to play the whole sixty minutes."

There was never any doubt in my mind that we could beat Gainesville. Yes, they had a roster filled with very good players. Junior running back Tommy West would later go to Tennessee on a full scholarship.

Before the big games, I would try to take our team's temperature by talking to Charles Turner and Al Cason.

I pulled Charles off to the side after Thursday's practice. He was quietly confident.

"Nobody outside of our locker room thinks we have any kind of chance to win this game," said Charles. "But look how far we have come. After we started 0–2, who thought we'd be here? They [Gainesville] are good. But we can beat them."

Al was beat up for most of the second half of the season, but there was no way he was missing this game.

"We just need to keep it close," he said. "The pressure is on them. They're supposed to be the better team and they are playing at home."

Coach Veazey gave us his pregame speech, telling us that it didn't matter how big the Gainesville team was or how many future college players they had.

"You deserve to be here," he said.

Then he pulled a newspaper clipping out of his pocket from the *Atlanta Journal-Constitution*. The writer was picking the playoff games for that Friday night and wrote that "Gainesville could name its score against Greene County."

Gainesville . . . . . . could name its score . . . . . . against Greene County.

Coach Veazey got angry and threw the clipping onto the floor of the locker room and stomped on it. And then we rushed onto the field and raced to the far end of the stadium, where we waited for Gainesville's team to come out of its locker room.

The door swung open and out came the Red Elephants. And they just kept coming and coming and coming. The roster in the game program said there were sixty-five Gainesville players. It looked like a hundred.

"I was standing there with Freddie Walker," said Tommy Moon. "I just said, 'Man, when are they going to stop coming out of their locker room?'"

Coach Veazey could see us staring at the Gainesville players. Not only were there a lot of them, but they were big, and they looked fast.

"Daddy pitched a fit," said Coach Veazey's son, Chartie, a manager on the team. "He yelled, 'Get them in the field house!'"

Many years later, when our teammate Arthur Jackson was a Georgia state trooper, he worked a security detail for a game in Atlanta involving Clemson. Tommy West, the rugged Gainesville running back, was by then Clemson's head coach.

West told Arthur that the whole episode of us watching Gainesville run out of their locker room had been set up.

"He told me that they waited to come out late on purpose so we would be watching," Arthur said. "They wanted to intimidate us."

"It worked," said Tommy Moon with a laugh.

They may have intimidated us in the pregame warmups. But not after the ball was kicked off.

We were having trouble moving the ball on the slippery surface in the first half.

"They were really big and really strong," said Charles Turner. "I tried to block Tommy West and I couldn't do it."

Right before halftime Gainesville put together a long drive, with Tommy West doing most of the work.

Miller Deaton, an all-state halfback, scored from six yards out with only twenty-four seconds left in the first half to give Gainesville a 7–0 lead.

We felt pretty good about things at halftime. Our defense was playing well against one of the best teams in the state. We just had to find a way to get some points on the board.

"At halftime, there was no doubt in my mind that we could play with those guys," said Tony Whittaker, our running back, who had a bad shoulder that night but played anyway. "We just needed to keep it close and hope to get some kind of break in the second half."

We finally put together a decent drive and got to the Gainesville thirty-yard line. But we couldn't turn the possession into points. We got pushed back to midfield and had to punt the ball away.

As the game went on, their depth and our lack of same began to show. We started getting tired.

"They kept running fresh guys at us," said Ben Allen Gresham. "We kept fighting, but we just wore down."

The backbreaker came when Gainesville's Charles Young took a punt on his own fifteen and ran seventy yards down the sideline to the Greene County fifteen-yard line. Five plays later, quarterback Joey Kinsey scored with 3:56 left to give Gainesville a 13–0 lead.

That was it. There would not be another comeback for the Greene County Tigers of 1970.

"They had a really good team, but we didn't let them push us around," said Tommy Moon. "Those guys knew they had been in a game."

We would find out later that Tony Whittaker played the entire game with a dislocated shoulder. He was in an incredible amount of pain.

"There was no way I was going to not play in that game," he said, his voice choking with emotion. "To go up there with as few guys as we had . . . everybody just played their hearts out."

As we walked off the field at Gainesville's City Park, we were hit with a reality that was colder than the late November night.

This was the last time the 19 of Greene would play football together.

"I can remember the feeling after the game," said Dennis Fordham, our assistant coach. "We played so hard. You could just feel the love that Coach [Veazey] had for us. It was one of those kinds of moments that sports is all about.

"Being a part of that team was one of the things in my life that I look back on and it feels good having been a part of it."

"It hurt. It hurt really bad," said Arthur Jackson when we met at his home in Stockbridge, Georgia. "What has it been? Fifty years? And I still remember how bad it felt."

Arthur, Charles Turner, and James Scott would all go on to play football at Clark College.

The rest of us seniors had been playing football since the seventh or eighth grade. And now it was over. We would never play in an organized football game again.

A historic journey that had begun in the warmth of spring practice had suddenly come to an end on a cold, damp, disappointing night in Gainesville. It left us with memories that we would still be talking about fifty years later.

It was a long bus ride home—a helluva lot longer than the ride up there, when everything was still possible.

In the painfully quiet darkness of the Greyhound bus, I could hear tears being shed. Some of those tears were mine.

8

MOVING ON

While we were heartbroken that our football season was over, a bunch of us—seven of us, in fact—were also on the Greene County boys' basketball team. We looked forward to playing together under Coach Dennis Fordham and Coach Benny Asbury.

The nine seniors among the 19 of Greene—Eric Ashley, Al Cason, Dene Channell, Arthur Jackson, James Scott, Edward Stapleton, Charles Turner, Freddie Walker, and me—felt that we had gone through the toughest part of the transition for Floyd T. Corry and Greene County High Schools. The 19 of Greene had done their part in bringing this new community together around a common purpose.

Now it was a matter of us each getting ready for the next chapter of our lives.

Some of our teachers, coaches, and administrators also decided that it was time to move on.

In advance of its merger with Toccoa High School in the fall of 1971, Stephens County High School offered Coach Veazey the job of head football coach and athletic director. The opportunity was too good for him to pass up.

On January 22, 1971, it was officially announced in the *Herald-Journal* that Coach Veazey was leaving Greene County. He was a Greensboro native who had been the school's head football

On January 22, 1971, the *Herald-Journal* reported that Coach Veazey
was leaving Greene County to take a job at Stephens County.
Photo courtesy of the *Herald-Journal*.

coach since 1962, when it was still Greensboro High School. He
told us the news in what was a very emotional team meeting.

Several weeks later, assistant coach Mack Poss, who was in his
fourth year at Greene County, announced that he was going with
Coach Veazey to Stephens County.

Tommi Ward, who for two years had played an important
role in the transition effort at Greene County High School, left
Greensboro to join her husband, Rick, at Fort Bragg, North Carolina, where he was stationed after returning from Vietnam.

On March 15, Ellis Foster, the principal who had led the new
Greene County High School through integration, announced
that he had tendered his resignation to the Greene County Board

of Education. At the end of the school year he left to become principal at Hart County Junior High School in Hartwell, Georgia.

On March 19, Evans Acree, who had been the principal at Union Point High in the 1960s, returned to Greensboro to become principal at Greene County High School.

On June 1, 1971, the largest senior class in the history of Greene County High School—113 students—received their diplomas at the school gymnasium. Of those seniors, 57 were black and 56 were white. The first fully integrated class had made it.

On August 6, John Gregory, who had served as guidance counselor at Greene County High School in 1970–1971, was announced as the school's new head football coach. Gregory had been an assistant coach at the University of Georgia from 1956 to 1963, after which he scouted for the NFL's Oakland Raiders.

Assistant football coach Larry Callair, who was considered to be a strong candidate for the head coaching job at Greene County, left to join the staff of Butler High School in Augusta.

And so life went on.

On August 27, the 1971 Greene County Tigers played their first game of the season against Putnam County.

The team had only sixteen players. They lost 16–6.

The 1971 team went 5–5 but won three of its last four games.

"We missed the seniors from the year before," said Tom Faust, an end on the 1971 team. "They had set a very high standard."

After the 1971 season, Tom Temple was named head football coach at Greene County, and he remained there for seventeen years, winning three region championships.

Temple was replaced by Charles Winslette, who had been a great high school player at Putnam County High School. Coach Winslette would win a state championship at Greene County in 1993.

There would be other periods of success for Greene County football. Larry Milligan served from 2002 to 2008, putting together a 13–1 season in 2004.

Winslette returned to Greene County in 2009 and stayed for three seasons before retiring with 260 career wins and two state

Ellis D. Foster, Resigns As Principal Of County High School

Greene County High School Principal Ellis D. Foster told the Herald Journal Monday March 15th that after this school term ends in June 1971, that he will no longer be Principal of Greene County High School, a position he has held since the beginning of Greene County High School in 1965. He has submitted his resignation to the Greene County Board of Education.

Mr. Foster came to Greensboro in 1949 and taught English and English Literature at Greensboro High School. He also coached Boy's basketball and had some of the best teams in the school history.

drowned during the Christmas holidays at Clark Hill on a duck hunting trip.

In the fall of 1965, Greene County High School was born, with the consolidation of Union Point and Greensboro High Schools. The Greene County Board of Education chose the Greensboro Principal, Ellis D. Foster, to be Principal of Greene County High School.

For the past 12 years, Mr. Foster has been in charge of Greensboro and Greene County High Schools. The schools have taken great strides in the fields of education, literary works and the success of a well-rounded athletic program.

The native of Demorest, Ga., is married to the former Miss Elaine Hunt of Demorest. They have three children Kathie 16, Phil 14, and Sandra 7.

The Foster family has been a credit to Greensboro and Greene County. They will be greatly missed by the wide circle of friends they have made in Greene County.

In the 22 years that Ellis Foster worked with the students and teachers in Greene County he left a mark of fairness. Teachers and students who served under him have learned to respect and love him.

The Herald Journal along with his many friends wish Mr. Foster the best success in the future. The 22 years that Ellis Foster spent in Greene County as a dedicated school man will leave a cherishing memory.

MR. ELLIS D. FOSTER

In January 1959, the Greene County Board of Education named the Piedmont graduate, Principal of Greensboro High School. Mr. Foster replaced the late Mr. Roy F. Burke who

The *Herald-Journal* reported on March 19, 1971, that Greene County principal Ellis Foster was leaving to take a job at Hart County Junior High School in Hartwell. Photo courtesy of the *Herald-Journal*.

championships. His other state championship was at West Rome in 1985.

Former University of Georgia star player Robert Edwards became head coach for six seasons (2012–2017).

In March 2018, Larry Milligan announced he was returning to Greene County as head coach. He went 9–3 and won a region championship in his first season back. After that, it became a struggle. In 2019, Greene County had a 2–8 record. In the COVID-ravaged season of 2020, the Tigers went 1–8.

In 2021, Greene County went 4–6. Terrance Banks took over as head coach in December 2021 following Milligan's retirement.

"There is not a better place to coach, which is why we came back," Coach Milligan told me in a phone conversation prior to leaving Greene County. "The kids here are special. They appreciate everything you do for them. This place will always seem like home to me."

We know what you mean, Coach.

9

THE PLAYERS

It has been more than fifty-two years since the 19 of Greene played their last game together on November 20, 1970.

As of this writing, fifteen of us are still alive. Gone are Edward Stapleton (cancer) and Freddie Walker (Alzheimer's disease), both of whom died in 2018. James Scott passed away from various health issues in 1995. James Kimbro also had an assortment of health issues before he passed away on May 31, 2022.

I interviewed all the living players. Twelve of those interviews were in person.

For a relatively small group of students, the 19 of Greene accomplished a lot after high school.

Charles Turner was the only member of our team to have a successful college football career, playing four seasons at Clark College in Atlanta. Charles also had great success as a high school coach and administrator, winning a state championship in girls' basketball. He belongs to four different Halls of Fame.

Tommy Faust served thirty years in the military, rising to the rank of colonel. He had another ten years of civilian service after that.

Al Cason was a hospital pharmacist for thirty-four years.

Arthur Jackson served as a Georgia state trooper for twenty-nine years.

Tommy Moon was a PGA golf professional for thirty-eight years.

I just completed my forty-sixth year of covering college football for newspapers, radio, television, and the internet. In May 2021, I was inducted into the Georgia Sports Hall of Fame.

Dene Channell followed in his father's footsteps and became a successful farmer who served on the Greene County Board of Education.

Here are the stories of the 19 of Greene.

ERIC ASHLEY (NO. 73)

Eric Ashley. Photo courtesy of Greene County High School.

Eric's parents, Billy and Mary Jean Ashley—I called them "Mr. Billy" and "Mama Jean"—were strong supporters of the Greene County public schools.

Mama Jean served as a substitute teacher at Greene County High School and was an advisor to the *Tiger*, the student yearbook, for the 1970–1971 school year. Mr. Billy was very involved in Greene County politics.

And they treated me like their third son, inviting me to University of Georgia football games, beach trips, and other family gatherings. Other than my own mother, Mama Jean was my biggest fan.

Eric's roots in Greene County High School ran deep. His older brother, Seaby, attended Greensboro High School and played on its football team. After graduation, he went on to the University of Georgia School of Law. Seaby died in 2001 after battling cancer. He was only fifty-three years old.

Because of his parents' involvement in education and local

Tony with Eric Ashley at Eric's home in Bogart, Georgia. Photo courtesy of Tony Barnhart.

politics, Eric said he was aware that Greene County High School was on the path to full integration by the fall of 1970.

"I knew what was coming down the pike," Eric said when we met at his home in Bogart, near Athens. "It was a discussion at our house at the dinner table. My brother was finishing up law school, so he knew what was going on. I was grateful for that knowledge."

"I knew how strongly Momma and Daddy felt about the public schools, but my parents gave me the option of going to NGA [Nathanael Greene Academy]," said Eric. "I never considered it."

Eric grew up in a little brick house on Main Street in Greensboro and was in the sixth grade when he and his family moved to 204 East South Street in Greensboro. It would be his parents' home for the rest of their lives.

In fact, the class superlatives photos in our 1970–1971 yearbook were taken at the Ashleys' house on East South Street.

Eric played varsity football for the 1969 and 1970 seasons. He played offensive and defensive tackle and was our placekicker as well.

At 6'3" and 185 pounds, Eric seemed to me to have had the physical frame to be a college football player at some level.

"I never had any inkling of playing college football, but after the Gainesville game, Coach Poss came into the locker room and said there was a scout from Presbyterian College [in South

Carolina] who wanted to see me," said Eric. "We talked, but it didn't work out. That's as close as I came to playing football again after that night in Gainesville."

After graduating from Greene County High, Eric enrolled at Georgia Southern College (now Georgia Southern University) in Statesboro, where he was stuck with me as a roommate at Sanford Hall in the fall of 1971. He became a dorm assistant as a junior, changed his major to finance, and graduated in the spring of 1975.

He went to work in Knoxville, Tennessee, and then moved to Athens, Georgia. In 1983, he went to work for Bradley Pontiac, an automobile dealer in Greensboro, which put him on the path to working for NAPA Auto Parts and eventually owning his own store.

Like most people, Eric has had his ups and downs in life.

Eric and his family built a house together on the Lake Oconee resort outside of Greensboro. But then Seaby got sick and passed away in 2001.

Eric went through a divorce in 2004. He lost Mama Jean in 2009. He and Joanna were married in 2013. Mr. Billy died on August 5, 2014, at the age of ninety.

Today, Eric owns a NAPA Auto Parts store in Greensboro and lives with Joanna in their lovely home in Bogart. He has six children and seven grandchildren.

"When I look back on the whole thing and how it developed, I know Seab never thought he would be the first to go," said Eric. "We thought we would be taking care of Momma and Daddy together. But I'm convinced the Lord always had a plan for me. There were a lot of good times as well as some sad times. But it's been fifty years and we're still here."

Eric said that going through the fall of 1970 and playing for the 19 of Greene was a net positive in his life.

"We were part of history. We didn't run from it," said Eric. "Being involved in it helped me over time.

"It really laid a foundation for the rest of our lives."

DAVID BARNHART (NO. 21)

David Barnhart. Photo courtesy of Greene County High School.

Like a lot of guys, my first real competitor in sports was my brother.

David was born on December 15, 1954, about sixteen months after me, and we competed in just about everything. No matter where we lived, we always had a basketball hoop, and some of our one-on-one games were epic. He didn't like to lose, and neither did I.

We had a Ping-Pong table on the back porch and would stay up late—much too late for my mom's liking—trying to beat each other's brains out.

For a while, my family lived near the elementary school in Union Point, just a few steps up Presbyterian Hill from the town's only tennis court. I remember the day my dad came home with his hands behind his back. He pulled out two wooden tennis rackets that he had purchased at Carlton's Hardware Store.

David and I both fell in love with the game and would spend hours at the tennis court. Our mother liked the idea that we were spending our free time playing tennis and not getting into mischief—although that was not always the case.

When I was a senior and David was a sophomore at Greene County High, we both made the tennis team. Mack Poss was our coach.

We both took up golf when a nine-hole course, the first in Greene County, was built just outside of Union Point in 1967. Mom helped us each order our first set of clubs from Sears & Roebuck.

We played on the same Little League baseball team—the Tigers. And we played basketball together on a team of sixth, seventh, and eighth graders in Union Point that a wonderful man named Charles "Red" Piland coached.

But our first love was football.

David and I played together on the 1970 team that won the Region 8-AA East Division championship.

"There were a lot of memories from that team," said David. "What I will never forget is that Freddie Walker had a long punt return for a touchdown when we played at Georgia Military College. He should have had another punt return for a score, but they called me for clipping on the play."

He paused for few seconds.

"And I DIDN'T clip the guy," he said with great conviction.

Like all the guys on our team, David will never forget our trip to Gainesville to play for the region championship.

"It was rainy and muddy, which pretty much nullified Freddie," said David. "He could have been the difference in the game."

After our 1970 season, David still had two seasons left of football. His 1971 Greene County team went 5–5.

"But we beat Morgan County, and that was our big rivalry game," he said.

His 1972 team went 6–4 under new coach Tom Temple, who would stay at Greene County for seventeen seasons.

David never left the Greene County/Morgan County area. Our dad owned his own construction company, and David got the building gene.

I didn't.

Today he is a field manager for a major construction company that builds exclusively at Lake Oconee.

David lost his wife, Toni, in 2015. He has three adult daughters—Valerie, Kelsey, and Bobbie Jean—and two grandchildren: Eli and Lucs.

TONY BARNHART (NO. 50)

Growing up in Union Point, I loved everything about football.

I vividly remember going to my first college game at the

Tony Barnhart. Photo courtesy of Greene County High School.

University of Georgia in Athens. Lois Cheves, mother of Becky (the first girl I ever had a crush on), took us to the Georgia-Vanderbilt game in 1965. It changed my life.

As a football player I was pretty average. When people ask me about my playing days, I always tell them, "I was small, but I compensated by being exceedingly slow."

Little did I know in high school that I would spend my entire career writing and talking about the game of football.

Truth be told, when I left Greene County for college, I wasn't quite sure what I wanted to be.

My English teacher at Greene County, Tommi Ward, was the first person to encourage me to think about writing as a profession.

"If you work at it, you could write for a living," she said, knowing that the operative word in that sentence was "work."

But I also had tremendous respect for all my coaches and the contributions they made to the lives of young people.

I always assumed I would go to college at the University of Georgia because it was only thirty-two miles from Union Point. But a number of Greene County graduates before me had gone to Georgia Southern. Coach Poss was a Georgia Southern graduate. They all urged me to visit the campus before I made my final decision. I fell in love with the place and enrolled for the fall quarter of 1971.

I started out as a physical education major, thinking I would teach and coach.

But one day I saw a notice on the bulletin board at Landrum Dining Hall. The *George-Anne*, the student newspaper, needed help in its sports department. I liked sports, and thanks to my mom and Tommi Ward, I loved reading and writing. So I gave it a shot.

The editor of the *George-Anne* sent me to a Georgia Southern basketball game. I wrote a story, and it appeared in the next edition with my byline. Those were my words on the page.

I was hooked.

I became sports editor of the *George-Anne* in 1973 and then transferred to Georgia to enter its School of Journalism (now Grady College). I eventually became the sports editor of the *Red & Black*, Georgia's student newspaper.

My first paying newspaper job was in Union, South Carolina (twenty miles east of Spartanburg), where I stayed for nine months. In March 1977, I moved on to Greensboro, North Carolina, where I stayed for seven and a half years. My wife, Maria—a Greene County girl—and I were married in the chapel of High Point (North Carolina) College, her alma mater, on August 14, 1977. Marrying Maria was the best decision I ever made.

Professionally, my big break came in August 1984 when I was hired by the *Atlanta Journal-Constitution*, where I stayed for twenty-five years.

In 1997, I branched out into television and became a reporter for ESPN's *College GameDay* show. I then spent eight years at CBS before joining the SEC Network in August 2014. In 2016, I was inducted into the Grady Fellowship at the University of Georgia, an honor which recognizes career contributions to the profession of journalism.

I was honored to be inducted into the Georgia Sports Hall of Fame on May 22, 2021.

Maria and I have lived in Dunwoody, Georgia, since 1994. In August 2022, we celebrated our forty-fifth wedding anniversary.

Our daughter (Sara Catherine), granddaughter (Sloane), grandson (Beau), and son-in-law (Brian) live close by.

I am one of the luckiest guys on the face of the earth. And it all started at Greene County High School.

AL CASON (NO. 22)

Al Cason. Photo courtesy of Greene County High School.

I know I'm not totally objective on the subject because I played with them, but I really believe Al Cason and Charles Turner are the two best athletes to ever play at Greene County High School.

Growing up, I spent a lot of time at Al's house, which was located on the road between Union Point and Greensboro. His parents, Grady and Martha, treated me as their other son. Al had two older sisters, Alice and Louise.

In the days before there was a lot of football on television, we would sit in Al's den and be quiet—very quiet—while Mr. Grady listened to the big game on the radio. Then we would go out into Al's yard and throw the football and pretend we were college players.

We had a lot of good running backs on our 1970 team at Greene County. But the reality is that in the second half of the season, when we won six of our last seven games to capture our division championship, a lot of our offense was built around Al Cason running the Green Bay Packers power sweep.

He took a pounding, which included suffering a separated shoulder in the last regular-season game. But he kept coming back and playing through the pain. He played the Region 8-AA championship game against Gainesville with a harness borrowed from the University of Georgia that would not allow him to raise his arm above his shoulder. Georgia running back Ricky Lake had used the harness in a big game against Auburn earlier in the season.

Given his skill and toughness, I thought Al was going to play college football somewhere. But during our conversation for

Tony with Al Cason at Al's home located between Milledgeville and Sandersville. Al was a pharmacist at Central State Hospital in Milledgeville for thirty-four years. Photo courtesy of Tony Barnhart.

this book, he made it clear that when he graduated from Greene County his body had had enough.

"I loved playing football, but I didn't like it when it took until Tuesday after the game to get the soreness out of my body," he said. "It was time for me to move on to something else."

He enrolled at Georgia College in Milledgeville, Georgia, and after two years transferred to the pharmacy school at the University of Georgia in Athens.

Back then, a pharmacy internship in the state of Georgia had to include work at both the retail level and the hospital level.

So Al served part of his internship at Central State Hospital (CSH) in Milledgeville, which at one point was among the largest facilities for the treatment of the mentally ill in the world. In the 1960s CSH had more than twelve thousand patients and some six thousand employees.

But then things changed when it came to caring for the mentally ill, who were no longer warehoused in places like Central State Hospital. Today there are only two hundred patients at CSH.

Al took me on a tour of the formerly sprawling campus, now filled with empty buildings and dilapidated houses where employees once lived.

Still, Al found a professional home there and retired from csh with thirty-four years of service as a pharmacist.

"I liked the atmosphere. It was more laid-back," Al said.

I spent a day with Al at his one-hundred-acre spread between Milledgeville and Sandersville, where he is growing a little bit of everything. We went through a bunch of newspaper clippings and memorabilia of the 1970 season that his mom had lovingly saved.

Then we watched videos of all our games. It was a great afternoon.

Al's favorite memory of our senior season?

Not far from where we had lunch in Milledgeville that day was Georgia Military College. Our Greene County team was 0–2 when we went to GMC on September 11, 1970. We beat them 28–12 and turned our season around.

"The coaches told us that if we won the game, we could swim in their pool," said Cason. "And so we did."

Al took a lot of pride in the fact that he lettered four years in varsity football and started for three. And he was a four-year starter in basketball. He also ran track for three years.

It was a great afternoon with Al—one that I will never forget.

DENE CHANNELL (NO. 12)

Dene graduated from Greene County High School in 1971 and returned home after graduating from West Georgia College in 1976. He would never leave Greene County again.

"I was born two miles from where I live right now," he said when we met at Festival Hall in Greensboro.

Dene's father, J. W. "Duck" Channell, was a terrific athlete who supplemented his income by playing baseball in the old Ogeechee League in the 1940s. That semipro league featured a lot of great players, including Charley Trippi, who was the runner-up for the Heisman Trophy at Georgia in 1946.

"Daddy made $35 a week working in the mill," said Dene. "But he made $50 a game playing baseball. Sometimes he would pitch doubleheaders and make $100 in a day. That was a lot of money back then.

"One night in Thomson [Georgia], he hit a grand slam home run. When he got back to the dugout, Momma handed him a hat full of money. The guys in the stands were betting on the game.

Dene Channell. Photo courtesy of Greene County High School.

"When they got engaged, he told Momma once he made $10,000 playing baseball they could get married.

"It didn't take long."

"Momma" was Dorothy "Dot" Channell, who taught mathematics to a couple of generations of Greene County children, including her son.

"She started in the 1940s as an English teacher, but Greene County didn't have an opening for an English teacher," said Dene. "So she went back to the University of Georgia and got a master's in math."

I can tell you this firsthand: Mrs. Channell was a great math teacher. She also did not put up with any foolishness in her classroom.

"She was very strict," said Dene. "I couldn't get away with anything. If I got into trouble at school, she would know about it in two minutes. One day a bunch of us walked into her classroom talking. She made us walk back out and walk in again."

Dorothy Channell passed away in 2006.

"My daddy didn't go to college, but he respected the fact that my mother had," said Dene. "He wanted me to go to college."

Dene graduated from Greene County High School in 1971, having lettered in four varsity sports: football, basketball, track, and golf.

Dene then graduated with honors from West Georgia College (now the University of West Georgia) in 1976.

Dorothy Channell, mother of Dene Channell, was a no-nonsense math teacher who cared deeply about her students. Photo courtesy of Greene County High School.

Dene Channell with Tony at Festival Hall in Greensboro. Photo courtesy of Tony Barnhart.

J. W. "Duck" Channell, father of Dene, was a member of the Greene County Board of Education. He also was an outstanding baseball player. Photo courtesy of Greene County High School.

Of all the lessons he learned from his father, Dene said that one of the greatest was to love the land. Dene could have been successful in whatever he chose to do after college. He chose to be a farmer.

When Dene married Kathy Perkins, his high school sweetheart, his father made him an offer.

"He said, 'I have 170 acres I can sell or give it to you,'" Dene told me. "He gave it to me, and we stayed in partnership until he died in 2007.

"I had good times with him. He was a good man. He treated me as well as anybody could treat a child."

Dene got involved in local politics and served two years on the Greene County Board of Education, just like his father. He also was elected chairman of the Greene County Board of Commissioners twice.

"I have no regrets," he said. "I'm glad I made the decision I made [to stay in Greene County]. Kathy didn't get to travel the world, but it all worked out."

GUY CRUTCHFIELD (NO. 62)

Guy, a junior guard on the 19 of Greene, turned out to be the one person on our team who chose to live a long, long way from Greene County.

As a senior, he played on the 1971 team that went 5–5. After high school, he joined the navy and was stationed in California.

Guy fell in love with the West Coast.

"Once I saw California, I made up my mind I was never going to leave," he said, when we talked by phone. "It was just so beautiful."

After he got out of the service, Guy attended Ventura College, located sixty or so miles northwest of Los Angeles.

He eventually went to work in a machine shop, and he enjoyed it so much that he stayed for almost forty years. He recently retired.

Guy Crutchfield. Photo courtesy of Greene County High School.

Like all the guys on the team I've interviewed, Guy could not believe that five decades have passed since our unforgettable 1970 season.

"There is a lot I don't remember from back then, but I'll never forget being on that football team," he said. "We didn't have a lot of players, but those we had needed to be in shape. All of us had to play on both sides of the ball."

Another memory that will last a lifetime, Guy said, was our 13–0 loss at Gainesville, which ended our dream season of 1970.

"We gave them a game. I know that," he said. "They didn't intimidate us. We never backed down."

Guy said that the lessons he learned about race relations and getting along with people in the 1970–1971 school year have stuck with him to this day.

"We all had to change. We all had to adjust. We tried something new. Nobody knew if it was going to work or not, but we made it work," he said. "I'll never forget that group of guys. We all came from different places, but we bonded. We'll always be a team."

Guy has been married twice.

In retirement, Guy has been working as a part-time preacher at the Calvary Missionary Baptist Church in Oxnard, California.

Guy said that when his mother was still alive, he would try to get back to Greene County every year or so to visit. But she is gone now. He came back for her funeral several years ago.

He still loves his West Coast home.

"Life is good. I have a great senior pastor who keeps me in check and helps keep me focused," he said. "I try not to live too fast now."

RICKY EASLEY (NO. 42)

Rick Easley. Photo courtesy of Greene County High School.

Dr. Charles Easley and his wife, Sylva, were heavily invested in the public schools of Greene County.

Dr. Easley, a very successful dentist, was a member of the Greene County Board of Education.

The Easleys' son Ricky, who was a junior on our 1970 team, was one of four brothers—Frank, Charles, and Sam were the others—who were educated at Greene County High School.

Ricky once asked his dad about leaving Greene County High and enrolling at Nathanael Greene Academy, the private school that would be opening its doors in August 1969. Ricky had heard that some of his friends were thinking about going to NGA, and he thought it might be a cool thing to do.

It was a short conversation.

"I should never have [brought it up]. He said no and told me to never mention it again," said Ricky, when we met at Festival Hall in February 2020. "Daddy just believed strongly in public schools. There was never a second thought about it."

Ricky was destined to be interested in sports. Dr. Easley was a football player and boxer at Presbyterian College in South Carolina. He boxed at Madison Square Garden before he enlisted in the army. Then there was dental school at Emory University. Dr. Easley followed in the footsteps of his father and practiced with him for a year.

Ford Boston, who would become superintendent of the Greene County School System, and Dr. Lee Parker, one of the most respected physicians in the county, were among those who convinced Dr. Easley to come to Greene County and set up his dentistry practice. He never left.

Dr. Charles Easley, father of Ricky, was a prominent dentist and a member of the Greene County Board of Education. He also was an outstanding athlete who once boxed at Madison Square Garden. Photo courtesy of Greene County High School.

Tony with Ricky Easley at Festival Hall in Greensboro. Photo courtesy of Tony Barnhart.

Dr. Easley was known by his friends as "Chic," while Sylva was "Mama Chic." And whenever a new couple moved into Greene County, Chic and Mama Chic would take them under their wing and make sure they settled in.

"I can't tell you how many times I heard that story," said Ricky. "Mama and Daddy cared about people."

Ricky noted that when the Floyd T. Corry players came over to Greene County High School in the fall of 1970, he and Ben Allen Gresham, a black running back, immediately became good friends.

"I know some people had some concerns about what it was going to be like when we integrated the schools," said Ricky. "I didn't because of the way my parents raised me. When I was growing up, anybody, black or white, was welcome in our home."

Ricky said he didn't play a lot on that 1970 team, but he does have some fond memories of that season.

"Al Cason was a great running back because he had such good body lean," said Ricky. "He was very hard to tackle."

"Tony Whittaker played with a bad shoulder most of his junior and senior years," said Ricky. "He was a tough, tough guy."

Like the rest of us, Ricky knew at first sight that Charles Turner was going to be a star.

"He was so confident. His stride was so smooth," said Ricky. "He was cool, calm, and collected on the field."

Ricky was a senior on the 1971 Greene County football team. After high school he attended junior college and eventually got into law enforcement. He was with the Greensboro City Police for six years.

With the building of the Lake Oconee resort in the 1980s, Ricky found that he had a knack for landscape design. Much of the landscaping work that you see today at the lake was done by Ricky and his company.

Today his son, Jimmy, helps run the business.

"It has been quite a ride," Ricky said, looking back on the past fifty years. "I've been blessed."

TOM FAUST (NO. 81)

Tommy Faust. Photo courtesy of Greene County High School.

As a member of a military family that traveled around the world, Tom had lived in diverse communities for his entire life by the time he and his family moved back to Greene County in 1970. So the fact that the schools were about to fully integrate "was no big deal."

"Everybody was talking about integration," he said. "I had grown up around black kids, white kids, Asian kids—all kinds of kids. I was an army brat who was used to growing up around a lot of other army brats. It wasn't good. It wasn't bad. It was just different."

Tom was a junior on the 19 of Greene team. But looking back, he remembers it being hard to focus on football that year because his father, Chief Warrant Officer Arlon W. "Jack" Faust, had been sent back to Vietnam.

"Personally, I don't think I gave my junior year my best effort," he said when we met at Festival Hall in Greensboro in October 2019. "During the season, he got his back broken in a noncombat accident. He also had a heart attack. I was worrying about that. I didn't get a lot of playing time, probably because I didn't earn it."

Still, Tom believes the lessons he learned from playing football at Greene County in 1970 and 1971 served him well once he embarked on a forty-year career of military and civil service.

"We practiced hard, and the coaches took us where we needed to go," he said. "And there were a bunch of good guys who came over from Corry—Charles Turner, Guy Crutchfield, James Scott. They were just good people.

"Were there problems? Sure, but we worked them out."

Tony and Tom Faust at Festival Hall in Greensboro in October 2019. Photo courtesy of Tony Barnhart.

While Tom did not get a lot of playing time in 1970, he said he'll never forget our trip to Gainesville to play for the region championship.

"I don't think I've ever been colder in my life than I was that night in Gainesville," he said.

Tom was an integral part of the 1971 Greene County team that went 5–5. By then his father had retired from the army, which allowed Tom to relax and enjoy his senior year.

"I got to play a lot, and I didn't feel any pressure about my future," he said. "I knew I was going to go into the military."

The results on the field and in school, said Tom, were mixed when the 1971 season came around.

"Coach Veazey and Coach Poss left. John Gregory took over as head coach. Coach Gregory was not Coach Veazey, but you didn't expect him to be," said Tom.

Tom graduated from Greene County High School in 1972. He attended the University of Georgia on an ROTC scholarship and graduated as a second lieutenant. He spent thirty years in the army as a military intelligence officer.

Tom was on assignment to the Pentagon in Washington, D.C., on September 11, 2001, the date of the terrorist attacks on the United States. He was headed out of his office to catch a bus to the Pentagon when the plane hit.

"I spent the rest of the day accounting for all of our army G-2 people and [making] sure they were okay," he said. "It was a crazy day."

He retired as a colonel in 2002 and then spent ten years in the U.S. government civil service. He was awarded the National Intelligence Distinguished Service Medal in 2013 and was inducted into the Army Military Intelligence Corps Hall of Fame in 2015. He formed his own consulting company, the TFaust Company, LLC, in 2014.

Tom left the Washington, D.C., area after retiring and moved to Texas in the summer of 2021. He still owns his parents' house and land in the Greshamville community between Greensboro and Madison, where his son, Chris, lives. Tom visits several times a year to reconnect with the community and the great folks who live there.

Here's a salute to Colonel Faust and his service.

BEN ALLEN GRESHAM (NO. 41)

They say that dynamite comes in small packages, and that was certainly true of Ben Allen Gresham.

He was generously listed on our roster as 140 pounds. Despite being small in stature, he was big—very big—in heart.

When we were putting together our team in the spring of 1970, we didn't have enough varsity players for a conventional spring game. So the coaches decided that the nineteen players we had would face a team made up of seniors from both Greene County and Floyd T. Corry who had played in the fall of 1969.

Ben Allen Gresham. Photo courtesy of Greene County High School.

That group of seniors included a running back named Andrew Barrow who was so big and powerful that none of us could tackle him. Nobody, of course, but Ben Allen, then a sophomore, and one of the seven players who joined the team from Corry.

"The only way to tackle Barrow was to go at him low," said our teammate Arthur Jackson. "Ben Allen was the only guy who could get low enough to get Barrow on the ground."

We lost that game to the seniors, but Ben Allen impressed everybody that night. He was going to be a big part of our season in the fall. The guy could flat play.

Our 1970 team had a bunch of really good running backs: Al Cason, Dene Channell, Freddie Walker, Tony Whittaker. Ben Allen could run with any of them. He had great speed and was strong enough to break most arm tackles.

"Being the smallest guy on the team just made me want to play harder," said Ben Allen when we sat down together. "We all wanted to make our team the best we could. I didn't want to be the one holding us back."

Ben Allen remembers how it didn't take long for the guys from two different schools to bond and form a cohesive unit.

"What I still think of today is how that team jelled quickly," he said. "We all knew that we had each other's backs. After spring practice, guys from both schools started becoming friends. And once we became friends, we were a pretty tough team to beat."

Ben Allen was a leader on the 1971 Greene County team that went 5–5 under a new coaching staff.

"There was just a lot of turnover from the year before," said Ben Allen. "We had a good quarterback in Tommy Moon, who replaced Charles [Turner]. But things just weren't the same."

Ben Allen was one of the most popular students at Greene County High School. As a senior, he was named Mr. Homecoming 1971.

After graduating in the spring of 1972, Ben Allen moved to Atlanta and attended Atlanta Area Technical School to study heating and air conditioning repair. After a couple of years, he joined the Keebler Company, a well-known cookie and cracker manufacturer, where he stayed for twenty-three years. He later went to work for Nabisco.

He now lives in Lithonia and has five children and ten grandchildren.

On October 28, 2019, Ben Allen, Charles Turner, and I went to Augusta to visit Larry Callair, our former assistant coach, who was confined to a wheelchair after a serious accident.

During that trip, Ben Allen reflected on what playing on the 1970 Greene County team meant to him.

"We were part of something special, and I will never forget it," he said.

"There was negativity outside the school, but our team brought the community together—more than it had ever been."

ARTHUR JACKSON (NO. 32)

Years ago, I was on the field at the old Georgia Dome in Atlanta, getting ready to cover a college football game. I felt a tap on my shoulder and turned to see a large man wearing the uniform of the Georgia State Patrol.

"You don't recognize me, do you?" he said.

It was Arthur Jackson, one of nine seniors on our 1970 Greene County team, and one of seven players to come over from Floyd T. Corry. He was working security for the game, something he often did.

"It was the fun part of the job," Arthur said when we met at his home in Stockbridge in February 2020.

Arthur said that at first he was apprehensive about the merging of Greene County High and Corry High.

Arthur Jackson. Photo courtesy of Greene County High School.

"It was just so new and different," he said. "I really didn't know what to expect."

He had grown up in a very strict environment in which missing school was simply not allowed. Arthur did it once at Corry and got caught by Coach Callair. He never did it again.

There were also chores to be done right after school.

At the time, he wondered how his life was going to change when he left Floyd T. Corry and enrolled at Greene County High.

"I thought it was going to be really bad when we integrated, but when I got there everything was fine," he said. "Some of us were worried that when the schools combined there would be so many players that some of us wouldn't get to play. It didn't turn out that way."

It didn't turn out that way at all, as our team had only nineteen players.

"I never understand why we didn't have more guys on our team," he said. "But football is not an easy game to play. There is a lot of work involved."

Arthur's journey from Greene County High School to the Georgia State Patrol was an interesting one.

Arthur was one of three seniors on our team (Charles Turner and James Scott were the other two) to enroll at Clark College to play football, with the help of William J. Breeding, a longtime teacher, coach, principal, and community leader in Greene County.

"We were thinking about going to Fort Valley State [in Fort Valley, Georgia]. They wanted [James] Scott and Charles, but they didn't want me," said Arthur. "Mr. Breeding had some pull at Clark and told them to take us all."

Arthur said he got frustrated during his freshman year at Clark and went home. Mr. Breeding talked him into returning.

"He said it wouldn't look right if I left without completing the first year, so I went back," he said.

Arthur suffered a knee injury in the fall of his junior year and had surgery the day after Thanksgiving. He decided to leave college and try something else.

He enrolled at Athens Technical College to study design.

Arthur Jackson and Tony at Arthur's home in Stockbridge, Georgia. Arthur was a Georgia state trooper for twenty-nine years. Photo courtesy of Tony Barnhart.

"For some reason, I wanted to design churches. I love those big glass windows in churches," he said.

James Scott, who had also left Clark by then, was working at the old Omni arena. His boss, a Clark graduate, offered Arthur a job as an usher.

"While I was at the Omni, I met a guy who was in charge of the ambulance service," said Arthur. "He told me the Georgia State Patrol was hiring."

At first, Arthur felt his temper was too quick for a job like that. But he changed his mind and decided he would give it a try.

"I thought I would give it a shot even though I had never owned a gun or carried a gun in my life," he said. "In fact, the only gun I had ever shot was my grandfather's shotgun."

After three attempts at the state patrol entrance exam, Arthur made the necessary grade and began his training.

His first assignment was in Athens.

"The boss told me that I didn't have to write everybody a ticket," Arthur said. "I needed to talk to people because they were going through stuff. I wrote a whole lot of warnings that year."

He had a bout with prostate cancer in 2004. The last eight years of his career, Arthur was assigned to the governor's mansion in Atlanta. He finally retired after suffering arthritis in his back.

"I was not going to put the governor at risk," he said. "That's when I knew it was time to go."

Looking back, Arthur said he learned a lot about life—and football—when he played with the 19 of Greene.

"I was young and a little scared," said Arthur. "Coach Veazey taught me different blocking techniques and difference stances. Coach Fordham taught me about angles.

"But when it was over, I remember having a conversation with [James] Scott. We just wished that group of guys could have had one more year together. It was a very, very special team."

MIKE JACKSON (NO. 80)

Mike Jackson. Photo courtesy of Greene County High School.

Mike was a junior on our 1970 team, and when we met at Festival Hall in February 2020, he admitted that he had had some serious reservations about the merger of Floyd T. Corry and Greene County.

"I wanted to finish high school at Corry because I was comfortable there," he said. "I was afraid at first because I didn't know how things were going to be between the races. I didn't know if I was going to be accepted.

"But after I got there, it wasn't as bad as I thought it was going to be."

Mike saw limited playing time on our East Division championship team in 1970 but was looking forward to being an important member of the 1971 team, with players like Tommy Moon, Ben Allen Gresham, Charles Martin, David Barnhart, Tom Faust, and Tony Whittaker returning.

But he said he missed part of preseason practice because of a summer job in Pennsylvania that allowed him to make his own money and buy his own clothes.

"I worked at a camp running a laundromat for three hundred campers," he said. "The money was good. I made myself proud and made my parents proud."

Mike lost some playing time early in the 1971 season because of the missed practice. But the coaches knew he was a pretty good wide receiver with excellent speed, and eventually he earned his way back into the lineup. He showed his speed as a senior when he ran a punt back eighty-five yards in a home game against Georgia Military College.

Mike Jackson and Tony at Festival Hall in Greensboro in January 2020. Photo courtesy of Tony Barnhart.

"Once I hit the sideline, they ain't seeing nothing but No. 80 [his number]," Mike said with a big grin.

"After that, [the coaches] told me I would be back there [fielding punts] for the rest of the season," he said.

Mike graduated from Greene County High in 1972 and then went to Durham Business College in North Carolina, hoping to study radio communications. He came back to Georgia five years later and moved to Barrow County with his wife. They eventually separated after sixteen years of marriage.

Today, Mike Jackson is back in Greensboro and says he has nothing but good memories of his final two years of playing for Greene County High School.

"The only thing I wish is that our 1970 team could have had one more year together," he said. "We really had some good ball-players—black and white. We could have gone somewhere."

Mike said he will always be grateful for the support that the teachers and coaches gave him his final two years at Greene County High School. He said the support gave him confidence during a difficult part of his life.

"What I will never forget is Coach Poss, who always would encourage me. He would always say, 'You the boy, Mike Jackson. You the boy!' I still remember him saying that. It made me feel good."

JAMES KIMBRO (NO. 70)

James Kimbro. Photo courtesy of Greene County High School.

James Kimbro always had his own special way of doing things.

Nicholas Antone, one of the coaches who came over from Corry High, found that out in the third game of our 1970 season, at Georgia Military College.

"James was our nose guard on defense, so he was supposed to be down on the ground on all fours," said Coach Antone. "But during the game, he came to me and said, 'Coach, can I just stand up with a two-point stance?' I didn't know if that was a very smart thing to do, but I just let him try. After he stopped them a couple of times, they didn't run up the middle for the rest of the night. James was like a windshield wiper cleaning things up."

James was one of three sophomores on our 1970 team. Very quick and athletic at 170 pounds, he started preseason practice as a member of the "B" team. But he was just too good of an athlete to keep off the field. So he was moved up to the varsity right before the season started.

Because of COVID-19, I interviewed James by phone in October 2020.

"I was excited because I didn't know if I was going to spend another season on the 'B' team," he said. "I also thought we were going to have a good team, and I wanted to be a part of it."

Like most of the guys I've interviewed for this book, James was concerned when we started the season by losing our first two games.

"But it felt like we were getting a little more confident in what we could do," he said.

Also like a lot of my teammates, James said that he will never forget our trip on the Greyhound bus to play the Gainesville Red Elephants for the region championship.

"It was wet. It was cold. And they dressed out what looked like eighty guys," James said. "They had a good team, but we had a good team too. We gave them everything we had."

After high school, James spent some time working in Atlanta.

"That didn't work out for me. I'm more of a country boy," he said.

He came back to Greene County and lived the rest of his life in Siloam, about six miles from our old high school. He passed away on May 31, 2022.

"Great guys and great coaches," James said. "I'll never forget them. It was a special time."

CHARLES MARTIN (NO. 64)

The 1970 Greene County team included three sophomores: David Barnhart, James Kimbro, and Charles Martin.

Charles had the perfect build for a fullback, but with only nineteen players on the team, we all had to be flexible. We had to play where we were needed.

"Coach Veazey came to me and said he needed a guard," said Charles, who now lives in Richmond, Virginia. "He said, 'I know

Charles Martin. Photo courtesy of Greene County High School.

you're a fullback, but I think you can handle the position. I promise next year we'll put you back in the backfield.'"

Charles learned early in his football career what the seniors on our team already knew: it was difficult to say no to Coach Veazey.

"I would do anything for Coach Veazey. I had grown up without a father, and Coach Veazey and Coach Callair helped me a lot. All the coaches offered a lot of encouragement."

So Charles Martin played the 1970 season at guard. And he was good.

"I never made it back to fullback," he said with a laugh.

Charles said that he was very impressed with Charles Turner, one of the seven players who had transferred from Floyd T. Corry.

"I will never forget the leadership of Charles Turner that year," he said. "And I will never forget the acceptance the black community gave me. It was something to emulate."

Charles admits that he was very disappointed when Coach Veazey and Coach Poss left Greene County for Stephens County after the 1970 season. John Gregory took over as head coach for the following season.

"It was low key and low energy," said Charles of the 1971 season. "I thought we had an opportunity to be a pretty good team. But it just wasn't the same. We had lost too many great leaders."

The 1971 team finished 5–5. The next season Tom Temple became head coach, and the team went 6–4.

Charles graduated from Greene County High in 1973 and enrolled at Georgia Southern. He spent two years there and then enlisted in the army in 1976. He returned to Georgia Southern and graduated with a bachelor's degree in technology in 1981. He worked with several companies, including cvs and Burger King, managing various construction sites.

Tragedy struck Charles's family in 1988 when his brother Ray, a former Greene County football player and 1970 graduate of GCHS, was killed in a parachuting accident.

Charles retired in 2015. He has two sons and one granddaughter.

"I'll never forget my time in Greene County, and I'll never forget that team," said Charles, who was voted Mr. Freshman in 1970. "I feel honored to have been a part of it."

TOMMY MOON (NO. 10)

Tommy Moon. Photo courtesy of Greene County High School.

Tommy has a distinction that few other football players can claim.

Generously listed at 170 pounds, Tommy was the starting center on our 1970 team. He was one of the team's best athletes, and that's where the need was.

The following season, his last at Greene County, he was the starting quarterback. And a very good one.

"You did what you had to do to help your team win," he said.

After our success in 1970, nine seniors and most of the coaching staff left. John Gregory, the new head coach, leaned heavily on Tommy in 1971.

"Coach Gregory would always ask me, 'Do you have the game plan?'" Tommy said with a smile. "I always told him I had the game plan."

Despite good play by Tommy and many others, Greene County finished 5–5 in 1971.

"We had lost too much talent and too many coaches," Tommy said.

Tony and Tommy Moon at Cherokee Run Golf Club in Conyers in 2020. Photo courtesy of Tony Barnhart.

He graduated from Greene County High School in 1972, unsure of what he wanted to do.

His life journey is among the most interesting ones from our 1970 team. After high school, Tommy went from the furniture business to the iron business, to hospital work in the army, to being a PGA golf professional for nearly four decades.

"When I left Greene County, I never thought that I would end up here," he said while we were having lunch at Cherokee Run Golf Club in Conyers, Georgia, where he had just retired from his position as director of golf. "It's been quite a ride."

Indeed, it *has* been quite a ride for Tommy Moon. He began the 1970 season as the No. 2 quarterback behind Charles Turner, but in the third game, against Georgia Military College, he was called on to play center because of an injury to our starter at that position.

"I might have been 170 pounds, and they put me up against a guy who weighed 273," he said. "I just kept going at the guy's feet to frustrate him. Finally he got so mad that he just picked me up and threw me what felt like forty yards."

Greene County won the game 28–12. It was our first win after starting 0–2. Tommy played center the rest of the season.

Tommy grew up in Union Point and began working at the Dairy Bar when he was only eleven years old for a dollar a day, plus tips. Sometimes he wouldn't get home until 12:30 a.m. He learned early that hard work would be a big part of his life.

"It's just what you did," said Tommy. "I had three brothers, and we all slept in one room."

Tommy also learned early in life that he loved to compete.

"I remember growing up playing ball on the playground at Union Point Elementary School," he said. "If you hit the ball on top of the gym, it was a home run. If you hit it in the tennis courts, it was a home run. I loved playing ball."

Tommy's life changed in 1975 when he joined the army. After basic training, he was sent to the army's Academy of Health Sciences at Fort Sam Houston in San Antonio, Texas. It was there that he got into the medical field, working in clinical chemistry at the base hospital.

"Mrs. Griffin, my high school chemistry teacher, would have been shocked," he said. "I was the worst chemistry student in the world."

By now he had married Nancy Thornton, a former Miss Greene County High School.

Another thing that changed Tommy's life was that, at the encouragement of his father-in-law, Dr. H. A. Thornton, he started getting serious about golf. After borrowing a set of old clubs from my brother, David, Tommy got some help from a teaching pro while he was based at Fort Sam Houston.

"I don't remember his name. He just agreed to help me," said Tommy. "It changed my life."

Then he was transferred to Fort Benning, near the Georgia-Alabama border. His job at the base hospital required that he work back-to-back sixteen-hour shifts, and then he'd get the rest of the week off. That left a lot of free time for the driving range. So he worked on his game. And worked. And worked.

And because of his natural athletic ability and his willingness to work, it didn't take long before Tommy became very good at golf.

In 1978, he made the All-Army team at Fort Benning, where he worked as an assistant to the club pro.

After leaving the army, Tommy took his G.I. Bill benefits and signed up for the PGA apprentice program. In 1985, he served a PGA apprenticeship at Springbrook Country Club in Lawrenceville, Georgia. In 1986, he moved to Honey Creek Golf & Country Club in Conyers, where he worked for twenty-three years and became the club's head golf professional in 1989. In 2010, he accepted the position of general manager and PGA golf director at Cherokee Run Golf Club, located within the Georgia International Horse Park in Conyers. He retired in December 2020.

He and Nancy have one grandson and three granddaughters.

"It's hard to believe it's been fifty years," he said. "When you look back at it, we did all right. We had a really good team made up of super guys. I just wish the group of guys we had in 1970 could have played one more year together."

JAMES SCOTT (NO. 74)

At 230 pounds, "Big Scott" was the largest member of our team. He was also one of the smartest.

James was one of the seven players who came over from Floyd T. Corry High for the fall of 1970.

"James was always the smartest guy in our group," said Charles Turner. "He was a big guy with a big heart."

The opening pages of our 1970–1971 high school yearbook include a photo of James sitting alone at Tiger Stadium, with only a one-word caption: "Solitude."

"Scott was an easygoing kind of guy," said Arthur Jackson.

He also was the best man at Arthur's wedding.

James Scott. Photo courtesy of Greene County High School.

After graduating from Greene County High, James attended Clark College with Charles Turner and Arthur Jackson.

Charles played all four years at Clark. James took another path. He worked security at the old Omni, a basketball and hockey arena in downtown Atlanta that no longer exists. He also managed a Church's Fried Chicken restaurant.

After a series of health problems, he died on April 17, 1995. He was only forty-three years old.

"I was only nine years old when he passed away," said Danielle Scott, his daughter and only child, who today lives in Athens.

James Scott was very close to his daughter, Danielle. He died in 1995 at the age of forty-three. Photo courtesy of Danielle Scott.

"He was a great dad," she said. "We had a lot of good father-daughter time. I can still hear the sound of his voice today. He was just a lovable guy."

Danielle's mom, Mildred Huff, remembered James as "nothing but a gentle giant. And Danielle looks just like his twin."

"He is truly missed," Mildred said. "He was just a wonderful man."

EDWARD STAPLETON (NO. 82)

Edward Stapleton. Photo courtesy of Greene County High School.

If there was ever a guy who was built—physically and mentally—to play a position, it was Edward Stapleton at defensive end for the Greene County Tigers.

"He was tough. Just incredibly tough," said Mack Poss, one of our assistant coaches. "It got to the point where other teams just didn't run in his direction."

Edward and his brother, George, played together at Greene County in 1969 when Edward was a junior and George was a senior. George and Edward lived only a couple of miles away from me in Union Point.

"He really enjoyed playing football, and he was really good at it," George said of Edward. "I just wish we had been able to play one more year together."

Edward played football with an intensity that rubbed off on the other guys. Every now and then a frustrated opponent would give him a cheap shot. That only made Edward play harder. If you were playing against Edward, you didn't want to make him mad.

After leaving Greene County, Edward started a career in the meat and grocery business. He would eventually retire from the

Edward Stapleton was a standout defensive end for the Greene County Tigers in 1970. He died of colon cancer in 2018. Photo courtesy of Greene County High School.

Great Northern Foods Company. He and his wife, Georgianne, moved to Lakeland, Florida.

Edward lost a son, Nick, in 2007, and his wife in 2011. In 2017, he was diagnosed with colon cancer. In July 2018, he moved to Blairsville, Georgia, to live with George.

"He died about three weeks after that," said George.

George still lives in Blairsville, where he retired after spending his entire career in the funeral home business. Edward and George's mother, Laura Stapleton Stewart, passed away in December 2020. Their sister, Libby Martin, lives in Greensboro.

CHARLES TURNER (NO. 11)

I first met Charles Turner in the spring of 1970 when he and a group of players from Floyd T. Corry High bused over to Greene County High for our first practices together.

At that point in my life, I did not have an African American friend. Little did I imagine at the time that Charles and I would still be friends fifty-two years later.

Two things were immediately clear about Charles:

1. He was going to be our starting quarterback for the 1970 season.
2. He was a born leader who was destined for success in whatever field he chose.

"Certain guys just have a presence about them," said Tom Faust, a junior on the 1970 team. "It was clear that the other guys from Corry saw him as their leader."

Charles Turner. Photo courtesy of Greene County High School.

Originally, Charles didn't want to play quarterback.

"I liked catching the ball," he said. "I wanted to be a receiver. I didn't know if I was good enough to play quarterback."

But the coaches knew.

And so did all the players.

"We knew before our first practice that we had a difference maker at quarterback in Charles Turner," said Coach Mack Poss. "The coaches at Corry told us he was special.

"And he was."

If there were any doubts about Charles being our quarterback, they ended after the spring game. We lost to the seniors from the season before, but Charles showed he had the running and throwing ability that gave us a chance to have a big season.

Charles grew up in a household that put a premium on hard work and discipline for both him and his sister, Janice. His mother, Chloe, was a schoolteacher for forty-three years. His father, Charlie, had his own floor-finishing business.

In the years before full integration came to Greene County, students were given the freedom of choice to attend Greene County High School or Corry High School.

Charles's sister enrolled at Greene County. Charles decided he would stay at Corry for his junior year in the fall of 1969.

"I'm sure sports had a lot to do with it," said Charles. "The group of guys I played with wanted to stick together."

During the 1969–1970 school year, Floyd T. Corry football and basketball coach Benny Asbury took Charles over to a basketball game at Greene County High School, where Charles first met football coach C. S. Veazey. Charles put on a coat and tie for the visit.

Tony and Charles Turner in Athens in 2019, at their first meeting to discuss this book. Photo courtesy of Tony Barnhart.

"Coach Veazey asked Mr. Asbury who he was bringing to Greene County next year," Charles recalled. "And he said, 'The best point guard you've ever seen.' To this day Mr. Asbury saying that still sticks with me."

In the fall of 1970, Charles would join his Floyd T. Corry classmates when their school merged with Greene County High to form the first completely integrated school in county history.

His mother had one piece of advice as her son prepared for his senior year in a new high school and a completely new environment.

"She just said, 'Do the right thing,'" said Charles. "My parents believed you should treat everybody fairly, and hopefully they will do the same to you."

As the quarterback of the newly integrated school's football team, Charles was in a very difficult position. It was important to the African American community in Greene County that Charles be the starting quarterback and that he be successful.

"Absolutely there was pressure on him," said Coach Nicholas Antone, who also came over from Corry. "But Charles never felt it. The coaches surrounded him. The players surrounded him. He was in that position at exactly the right time."

After graduating from Greene County High School in 1971, Charles accepted a scholarship to play football at Clark College (now Clark Atlanta University).

"The people at Clark told me that if I would come, they would take Jack [Arthur Jackson] and [James] Scott too," Charles said. "So that's what we did. Mr. [William J.] Breeding had a lot of pull at Clark and put that together."

Arthur Jackson attended Clark for two years and then left to become a Georgia state trooper. James Scott left after one year.

But Charles stayed at Clark and earned his degree.

He remembered the day that Coach Veazey and Coach Poss drove from Greensboro to Atlanta to watch him play for Clark College.

"That really meant a lot to me," said Charles.

After a successful playing career at Clark, Charles earned a free-agent tryout with the Dallas Cowboys.

In Thousand Oaks, California, in the summer of 1975, Charles looked around to see himself on the same practice field with Roger Staubach, Billy Joe DuPree, Dan Reeves, Lee Roy Jordan, and a bunch of other Cowboy greats.

The Cowboys were looking at Charles as a possible wide receiver.

"It was awesome," he said. "The only guy I couldn't beat was [cornerback] Mel Renfro. He was like glue. I was naïve enough to think that I could actually make the team."

After three weeks of living the dream, head coach Tom Landry delivered the bad news. Charles was not going to play for the Dallas Cowboys.

His football playing career was over.

"Most of the guys who got released didn't know what they were going to do next," he said. "But I had a degree. I knew what I wanted to do."

And thus he began a long and distinguished career as a coach and athletic administrator.

In addition to earning his undergraduate degree from Clark College in 1975, Charles also earned a graduate degree in 1999 from the United States Sports Academy. He became a Certified Athletic Administrator in 1996 and a Certified Master Athletic Administrator in 2003.

He began his coaching career at Oglethorpe County High School in 1975 and ended it in 2004 at Cedar Shoals High School in Athens.

During Charles's tenure as coach of the Cedar Shoals girls' basketball team, the school made four appearances in the state championship game, winning one state title. He also served with distinction as director of athletics at Cedar Shoals.

Charles is in the Clark Atlanta University Athletic Hall of Fame, the Cedar Shoals High School Hall of Fame, the Athens Athletic Hall of Fame, and the Georgia Athletic Directors Association (GADA) Hall of Fame. He is a former president and board member of the GADA.

After retiring from Cedar Shoals in 2004, Charles started his own sports marketing business. He lives in Statham, Georgia, with his wife, Cynthia. They have three adult children and six grandchildren.

In October 2022, Charles was one of the inaugural inductees into the Greene County Tigers Ring of Honor

FREDDIE WALKER (NO. 20)

Freddie's obituary said it all: "Freddie's career was in sales and sharing his infectious smile."

"My brother was a great guy," said Barry Walker, who was four years younger than Freddie. "People really liked him. He could

Freddie Walker. Photo courtesy of Greene County High School.

Freddie Walker had quick feet and a quick smile. In the fall of 1970, he was one of the best punt returners in Georgia. Freddie died in 2018 after a long battle with Alzheimer's disease. Photo courtesy of Greene County High School.

sell anything to anybody. He loved people and he loved life."

Freddie, said Barry, had a restless streak about him.

"It seems like Freddie worked fifteen different jobs when he got out of high school," said Barry. "He could talk and sell anything to anybody. He was a natural born salesman."

Freddie was slight of build (about 160 pounds) but had blinding speed. As a senior at Greene County High School, he won the region championship in the 100-yard dash.

He was especially dangerous as a punt returner. He had a long punt return for a touchdown in our first win of the season against Georgia Military College.

Later in the season, he returned a punt fifty-five yards for our only touchdown in a 7–6 win against Franklin County. He caught a fifty-two-yard pass for a touchdown against Stephens County. Opponents didn't believe how fast Freddie was until it was too late.

"Once Freddie got up to full speed, nobody could catch him," said Tommy Moon.

"Anytime I would see Freddie, I would tell him that he was the fastest white boy I ever saw," said Coach Nicholas Antone with a smile. "I would tell his wife, too. He was a special player for us."

In 1971, Freddie married Julie Brook. They had one child, a son.

In 1981, he married Susan Webb, who brought two sons into the marriage.

Freddie had seven grandchildren.

In 2011, Freddie was diagnosed with Alzheimer's disease. He died on October 4, 2018, at the age of 66.

According to his obituary, Freddie was an avid outdoorsman who enjoyed dirt bikes, golf, hunting, and fishing.

"Once you met Freddie, you would never forget him," Barry Walker said. "He was a special guy. I still miss him a lot."

TONY WHITTAKER (NO. 40)

Tony Whittaker. Photo courtesy of Greene County High School.

Tony was one of four Whittaker brothers who played football for Greene County High School. (Lynn, Andrew, and Richard were the others.)

He was a junior running back on our 1970 division championship team and played a very important role that year, despite nursing a bad shoulder for most of the season.

"That was a special team," said Tony, who still lives on the family farm in Greshamville, just outside of Greensboro.

When word came that Greene County High School would be fully integrated in the fall of 1970, Tony said that people tried to get him to enroll at the private school, Nathanael Greene Academy, that opened in August 1969 and was hoping to field its first football team.

"I said no," he said. "Greene County was my school. It's where my brothers played."

Tony with Tony Whittaker at Festival Hall in Greensboro in 2020. Photo courtesy of Tony Barnhart.

As it turned out, Nathanael Greene did not begin its football program until the fall of 1973.

Tony had dislocated his shoulder for the second time that season right before we got on the Greyhound bus to travel to Gainesville for the Region 8-AA championship game. It was one of the biggest football games in the history of Greene County High School.

"There was no way I was going to miss that game," he said. "I didn't care how bad it hurt."

Tony still gets emotional when he thinks of our 13–0 loss to Gainesville, which was the last game for our nine seniors.

"Everybody played their hearts out," said Tony. "I still think we were one of the best teams around. And nobody can tell me different."

Tony came back to Greene County High School for his senior season in the fall of 1971. But with the loss of nine seniors and a complete change in the coaching staff, things were just not the same.

"The difference between my junior season and my senior season was like night and day," he said.

Despite a couple of small college offers, Tony decided he would not try to play college football. He was done. His body had taken too much of a pounding.

"I had had two shoulder surgeries," he said. "There was no way it was going to hold up. It was time to move on."

After high school, Tony worked for the Georgia-Pacific Corporation. He also spent many years with a swimming pool chemical company in Conyers.

He never left the family's place in Greene County.

"I was born and raised here," he said. "I never wanted to go anywhere else. I've got no regrets."

10

THE COACHES, ADMINISTRATORS, AND TEACHERS

COACHES

Charlton S. Veazey, Head Coach

I was very young when I first met Coach Veazey. One of his summer jobs was to teach swimming lessons at the pool located between Greensboro and Union Point. I remember that he was patient with me because I was flat-out scared to be in water that was over my head.

But when I became a football player for him, I learned something very quickly: C. S. Veazey *the coach* had an edge. He was very competitive and believed that good results followed hard work just as surely as night follows day. He was a second father to me.

This quote from my teammate Eric Ashley perfectly sums up how we players felt about our coach: "Coach Veazey had a way about him that some people didn't like, but when you got to know him you realized he had a very big heart."

Coach Veazey knew that he had inherited a delicate situation when he was named head football coach of the combined Floyd T. Corry and Greene County High Schools. But it didn't change the way he coached his first racially integrated team. For my money, the powers that be in Greene County could not have selected a better man for the job.

Coach Callair, Coach Veazey, and Coach Poss discussing strategy at
Tiger Stadium. Photo courtesy of Greene County High School.

"Throughout the whole process [of integration], he had the
inner strength to make sure that it went the way it needed to go,"
said Eric Ashley. "I respected him tremendously."

"Daddy wanted to build up young men," said his son, Chartie,
who was a manager on our 1970 team. "He didn't care if they
were black or white. He wanted to make them the best football
players and the best men they could be."

"All of the players who came over from Corry respected Coach
Veazey," said Charles Turner. "Yes, he pushed me and got onto
me when I would do something wrong. But it made me a better
player. And it eventually made me a better coach."

Nobody could question Coach Veazey's credentials. He was

only sixteen years old when he enlisted in the navy in October 1941. About two months later came the attack on Pearl Harbor, and the United States was at war.

After the war, Coach Veazey came back to Greene County and earned his high school diploma in 1947. He then married hometown girl Eugenia Stanley and attended the University of Georgia, where he served as a trainer on the football, basketball, and baseball teams under coaches Wally Butts and Jim Whatley.

He began his teaching and coaching career in 1953 at LaGrange High School and eventually made his way back to Greensboro High School, where he was named head football coach in 1962. Greensboro High and Union Point High combined in 1965 to form Greene County High School.

That's when Tiger Stadium was built, and Coach Veazey did everything in his power to make the new stadium sparkle. He would cut the grass, line the field, and make sure the sprinklers were turned on at midnight to keep that beautiful grass looking like a carpet.

"If Daddy was down there [at the stadium], I was down there too," said Chartie. "I just wanted to be with him."

Our 1970 team was the last one he would coach at Greene County High School. When the season was over, he was offered the job of head football coach and director of athletics at Stephens County High School in Toccoa.

Coach Veazey and his wife, Gene, had raised three children (Chartie, Lynn, and Jeanie) in Greene County. Leaving was one of the most difficult decisions he ever had to make. He had led the Greene County High School football team through a difficult transition and got it to the region championship. But the offer from Stephens County was too good to pass up.

"It was a bittersweet time," said his daughter Lynn. "Mother and Dad were both native Greene Countians, and as a family, we had never moved. The home where we lived had belonged to my grandmother, and she moved out and gave it to them when they came back from LaGrange. It was the only home we had ever known."

Coach C. S. Veazey and his wife, Gene, were honored for the lifetime of service that they gave Greene County. Photo courtesy of Lynn Veazey Bowers.

"For Daddy, it was a welcomed challenge," said Chartie. "He had brought two schools together before, and here was another chance to do it."

He coached four seasons at Stephens County. He was 9–2 in each of his first two seasons and then went 3–6–1 and 3–7.

"Stephens County ended up being a tough road," said Lynn. "We went through some unexpected things during those last two seasons.

"There was a petition to get rid of him. We had kids rolling our house [with toilet paper] and putting 'For Sale' signs in the yard. Even though it wasn't a fun time, the blessings came from our friendships with some lovely people while we were there, and also later when God used those experiences for our good," said Lynn.

He coached four seasons at Wilkinson County High School after leaving Stephens County. In 1976, he won ten games and a region championship. His 1977 record was 8–2–1. In 1978, he went 3–6–1 and decided he was done.

The Veazeys returned to Greene County and built a house but

ultimately didn't retire. Mrs. Veazey continued to teach. Coach Veazey became the Greensboro city manager, a job he held from 1980 until 1991. Later, he was elected to the Greene County Board of Education for a term.

In 1999, C. S. and Gene Veazey were honored as "Citizens of the Year" for their volunteer service to the community and their combined forty-four years of experience teaching and coaching the youth of Greene County.

Those of us who played for Coach Veazey knew that at times he could be tough. But he was always fair.

"With Daddy, it was either right or it was wrong," said Lynn. "Many people adored him, but some didn't appreciate his forthright manner. He sometimes ruffled feathers with his candor, but he always had your best interest in his heart and in his mind."

What the folks who hated him didn't know about was all the kind acts he and Gene performed behind the scenes.

"When one student who had been particularly helpful with the team went off to college, Daddy and Mother bought a suit for him to wear for special occasions," said Lynn. "They did lots of things for their students. Some of them they never told us about. Our parents were quiet givers."

Eric Ashley told me of a run-in with Coach Veazey that got personal.

"In practice, I was loafing in front of everybody," said Eric. "Coach jumped up and got in my face and said, 'You couldn't carry Seaby Ashley's jockstrap!'"

Seaby was Eric's older brother, who played for Coach Veazey and then went on to law school.

"It made me mad," said Eric, who went on to tell me that he eventually understood that Coach Veazey was trying to make him a better person and a better player.

Eric said he went to see Coach Veazey near the end of his life.

"He couldn't speak, but he could smile," said Eric. "He seemed so grateful, and I will always remember that.

"I will always remember Coach Veazey as a good man who was doing the best he could. I loved him."

Coach Veazey died on October 5, 2011, at the age of eighty-five. I was honored to speak at the funeral at the First Baptist Church in Greensboro on behalf of his former players.

C. S. and Gene Veazey were married for sixty-three years. Gene died on December 20, 2019, at the age of ninety.

Coach Veazey has been gone for over ten years, but his spirit lives on in his players and his coaches.

Dennis Fordham played for Coach Veazey and then was an assistant coach under him.

"He was the kind of man who made you want to play for him," said Coach Fordham. "We would run through a wall for him because we knew that he would run through a wall for us."

"He was the perfect role model for me as a young coach," said Mack Poss, who joined Coach Veazey's staff at Greene County High School in 1967. "When I got to Greene County, I ate every meal at Coach Veazey's house until I got to the end of the summer. When school started, I ate in the lunchroom and went home with him for supper.

"He gave me a chance."

Coach Veazey gave a lot of us a chance to succeed as men, husbands, and fathers. He taught us discipline. He taught us determination. But most of all, he taught us to respect and love those around us. And for those life lessons, we are all eternally grateful.

We love you, Coach. We will never forget you. You will always be our coach.

Coach Nicholas Antone

Nicholas Antone was one of four African American coaches who came to Greene County High School from Floyd T. Corry. The others were Larry Callair (football, wrestling), Benny Asbury (football, boys' basketball), and Nathaniel Whitehead (football, girls' basketball, track).

"It was an outstanding group of coaches who came over from Corry," said Mack Poss, who was already an assistant at Greene County when the two schools merged.

In addition to his coaching duties, Nicholas Antone was a very popular English teacher in the new Greene County High School. Photo courtesy of Greene County High School.

A graduate of Alabama State College in Montgomery, Coach Antone came to Floyd T. Corry in 1966. And when the coaching staffs of Greene County and Floyd T. Corry merged in the spring of 1970, Coach Antone was given an interesting assignment.

We had only nineteen players on the varsity team—not enough to hold a traditional spring game. So it was decided that the varsity would play a team made up of seniors who had played for both schools the previous fall.

Coach Veazey asked Coach Antone to coach those seniors in the spring game.

Nicholas Antone and Tony at Mr. Antone's home in Greensboro. Photo courtesy of Tony Barnhart.

Behind a burly running back named Andrew Barrow, the seniors beat us.

"I just remember people standing up and cheering," Coach Antone said. "Some people wanted Greene County to win, and some wanted the seniors to win. What I knew after the game is that we were going to have a good team in the fall."

He turned out to be right.

Coach Antone was a teacher and coach at Greene County for four more years after our successful 1970 season. He then went to Hancock County, where he served as an administrator for twenty-eight years before retiring and returning to Greene County. He stayed retired for "about seven months" before Greene County High School called him back into duty.

"This is home," he said.

While he was a good coach for us, Coach Antone's biggest contribution to the success of integration at Greene County High School, in my opinion, came in the fall of 1969, the year before the schools were fully integrated. Students from Greene County were bused over to Floyd T. Corry, where two teachers from each school—including Coach Antone—taught fully integrated English classes. (Chapter 3 of this book tells a more complete story of that year.)

Coach Antone said he will always look back fondly on the 19 of Greene and the contributions everybody made during a difficult time.

"I definitely felt we did okay back then and feel the same way today," he said.

Coach Larry Callair

When I met Coach Larry Callair in the spring of 1970, he was a bear of a man.

I remember him opening the trunk of his car, which contained his own football equipment. He played semi-pro football with the Atlanta Packers and the Augusta Eagles for a grand total of $100 per game.

A native of Easton, Pennsylvania, Coach Callair came south when he was offered a football scholarship to play at South Carolina State in Orangeburg.

"I had a high school teammate [Billy Houston] who went to South Carolina State ahead of me," explained Coach Callair. "He said, 'Hey Larry, I need somebody to block for me.' And he got me a scholarship."

When he left South Carolina State, Coach Callair didn't want to go back to the cold of Pennsylvania. So he worked as a coach at a couple of Georgia high schools before landing at Floyd T. Corry in Greensboro. He was named as a varsity coach when Corry and Greene County merged in 1970. He also coached the wrestling team. He would cut hair on the side to earn some extra income.

Coach Larry Callair played football at South Carolina State and also played semi-pro football for the Atlanta Packers and the Augusta Eagles. Photo courtesy of Greene County High School.

On October 29, 2019, almost fifty years since we had last seen Coach Callair, Charles Turner, Ben Allen Gresham, and I went to visit him at his home in Augusta. Due to a riding mower accident, he was confined to a wheelchair. But he was all smiles and was thrilled that his old players would come to see him.

"We only had nineteen guys, but the ones that were worth their salt were the ones that decided to stay," he said during our visit. "It was a great group of guys. I remember going to Gainesville and those folks making fun of us because our team was so small. But we gave those guys all they wanted and then some."

But Coach Callair pulled no punches when it came to coaching his players. It didn't matter what race the player was. He would not back away from his expectations.

"Al Cason [who was white] and I locked heads one time," said Coach Callair. "So we had a meeting. Just the two of us. I told him I didn't care what color his skin was. I told him, 'I just want you to do the job and you'll get the position.' We never had a problem after that."

After the 1970 season, Principal Ellis Foster, Head Coach C. S. Veazey, and Assistant Coach Mack Poss all left Greene County for other jobs.

Tony, Ben Allen Gresham, and Charles Turner went to visit former Greene County assistant coach Larry Callair in October 2019. Coach Callair was confined to a wheelchair due to a lawn mower accident. Photo courtesy of Tony Barnhart.

"Mr. Foster told me that if he had stayed [at Greene County], I was going to be the head coach," Coach Callair said. "But he found a position for me at Butler High School in Augusta, where the principal was his friend."

While our visit meant a lot to Coach Callair, I promise that Charles, Ben Allen, and I got a lot more out of it.

"The thing I will always remember is how our team brought the whole county together," said Coach Callair. "The football team figured out a way to work together for the common good. The folks in our county realized they could do the same."

He kept coaching until his accident. Even after that, he still worked out several times a week. He told us that he was determined to get back on his feet.

He never did. Coach Callair passed away on January 8, 2023.

Coach Dennis Fordham

Dennis Fordham was an outstanding student when he played football and basketball and ran track at Greensboro High School. He went on to the University of Georgia, where he was a triple jumper on the track team.

After he graduated from Georgia in 1968, Greene County High had an opening for a teacher and coach. It was an opportunity to go home and work for his former coach, C. S. Veazey, and Principal Ellis Foster.

"My father left my family when I was a [high school] junior, and even before that Coach Veazey had basically adopted me," said Coach Fordham. "Both Coach Veazey and Mr. Foster had a tremendous influence on me."

He came to Greene County in the fall of 1968 as a math and science teacher, assistant football coach, and track coach. During the 1969–1970 school year, he became the boys' head basketball coach. Benny Asbury became the assistant boys' basketball coach at Greene County when he came over from Floyd T. Corry.

Coach Dennis Fordham was Coach Veazey's first all-state player. He left coaching after the 1970 season and became a successful public school administrator. Photo courtesy of Greene County High School.

Coach Dennis Fordham and Tony at Coach Fordham's home in Covington. Photo courtesy of Tony Barnhart.

Coach Fordham worked on his master's degree in math in the summers. With the Vietnam War still raging, he got a draft deferment because he was teaching.

In 1970–1971, Coach Fordham's main football duties were to coach the "B" team and then go on the road each Friday to scout the next team that Greene County would play.

Because he was always scouting the following week's opponent, Coach Fordham did not get a chance to see our team play until that night in Gainesville, the 19 of Greene's last game.

"We played so hard," Coach Fordham said of that 13–0 loss. "There was just great heart on that team. I am still proud to have been a part of it."

When Coach Veazey, Coach Poss, and Principal Foster left after the 1970–1971 school year, Coach Fordham decided to enter the doctorate program for mathematics education at the University of Georgia. He would not coach again.

But that decision launched him on a successful career in education and administration. He would retire in 2006 as the Hall County superintendent of schools.

I love this story:

Coach Fordham was the captain of Coach Veazey's first Greensboro High School team in 1962. The following season he became Coach Veazey's first all-state player.

From that point on, Coach Veazey kept a picture of Coach Fordham with that designation on the wall of his office.

When Coach Veazey passed away in 2011, his wife, Gene, gave the photo to Coach Fordham. It now hangs on the wall in his home office in Covington, where he lives with his wife, Andrea.

Coach Mack Poss

Mack Poss was a senior at Georgia Southern College in Statesboro in the spring of 1967. He was studying for a kinesiology test when the phone rang just down the hall from his dormitory room. It was a long-distance call, and back then getting a long-distance call was a big deal.

"I'll never forget the deep voice when he said, 'This is Charlton Veazey at Greene County High School,'" said Coach Poss when we met at his home in Toccoa.

With his graduation coming up, Coach Poss had been applying for teaching and coaching jobs all over Georgia and South Carolina. At that point, he had only one offer, from a high school in Hartsville, South Carolina.

Among the many letters Coach Poss had sent out was one to Charlie Davidson, a very successful coach at Washington-Wilkes High School in Washington, Georgia. Davidson didn't have an opening, but he passed Coach Poss's name along to one of his best friends in coaching, Charlton Veazey, when the two saw each other at a track meet.

"Charlie said you were interested in a teaching and coaching job, and I've got one," Coach Veazey said.

Coach Poss played on the Georgia Southern tennis team and had a match scheduled on Saturday. The next day, he drove from Statesboro to Greensboro to interview for the job. He met with Coach Veazey and Principal Ellis Foster. They offered him the job that day and asked that he make a decision as soon as possible.

Assistant football coach Mack Poss was very successful as a girls' basketball coach at Greene County High and Stephens County High. Photo courtesy of Greene County High School.

"My daddy rode up there with me, and as we were driving home, he asked me what I thought. I told him it [Greene County] was a lot closer to Momma's biscuits than Hartsville, South Carolina."

Coach Poss is a native of Lincolnton, Georgia, only forty-seven miles from Greensboro.

As soon as Coach Poss and his dad arrived at their home in Lincolnton, he called Coach Veazey and accepted the job.

Coach Poss was in his fourth season at Greene County High School when it merged with Floyd T. Corry.

"I just remember the mood as being upbeat," he said. "We were told there were some very good linemen [at Corry] and that we were going to get a gifted athlete who would probably be the starting quarterback."

When the unforgettable 1970 season was over, Coach Poss had a feeling that Coach Veazey would be leaving for Stephens County, and he had made it clear to Coach Veazey that he would like to go with him. But it was a hard decision for Coach Veazey.

"He had tears in his eyes when he said, 'This [Greene County] is my heart,'" said Coach Poss. "All he ever wanted to do is be the head coach at Greene County."

Coach Poss and Coach Veazey would stay together for four more years at Stephens County. But after successive seasons of 3–6–1 and 3–7, they were let go.

"We just didn't win enough games," he said.

Coach Veazey left for Wilkinson County, located in Central Georgia, and Coach Poss stayed at Stephens County to coach girls' basketball. In 1984, he left coaching to start his own investment firm, Mack Poss & Associates, which is still running strong today.

Coach Mack Poss and Tony at Coach Poss's home in Toccoa in 2020. Photo courtesy of Tony Barnhart.

He spent sixteen seasons as a radio commentator on the University of Georgia women's basketball broadcasts and is still active on local radio, doing a tailgate show for Stephens County football.

But part of him, he said, will always be with the Greene County Tigers of 1970.

"I will never forget it," he said. "What happened that season was a testament to all the players and the coaches on that team. It was special."

Coach Benny Asbury

Benny Asbury was educated in Greene County and then attended Morehouse College and Atlanta University. He also did academic work at Savannah State, Georgia College, and the University of Georgia.

After a stint in the armed services, he returned to Greene County, where he was an educator for thirty-five years. He served on the Union Point City Council for twelve years. He also served on the Greene County Board of Commissioners, the first African American to do so, and was vice-chair of the board for almost nineteen years.

In addition to coaching football and boys' basketball at Greene County High School, Mr. Asbury also taught physical education and driver's education.

"Mr. Asbury lived in Union Point and had to pass by my house to get to work in Greensboro," said Charles Turner. "I wish I had a dollar for every time he would pick me up for practice. I would be quite wealthy now. We weren't able to attend camps or just didn't know about them, but Mr. Asbury would always have basketball games scheduled with someone."

Coach Asbury married the former Carol McLemore, the long-time music and chorus teacher at Corry. They had a daughter, Chalise.

He passed away on September 14, 1999.

In addition to working as a coach and administrator for thirty-five years, Benny Asbury also served on the Union Point City Council. Photo courtesy of Greene County High School.

Coach Nathaniel Whitehead

Coach Whitehead was the head girls' basketball coach and track coach at Corry High School before he came to Greene County High, where he was the assistant girls' basketball coach, assistant football coach, and track coach.

Charles Turner remembers that Corry didn't have a regulation track but that Mr. Whitehead would measure out the distances so that the guys could work out.

Mr. Whitehead was a graduate of Tuskegee University.

He had a son, Nathaniel Jr., and a daughter, Sandra, who were both athletes and Greene County graduates. Nathaniel Jr. excelled in football, and Sandra served as the head girls' basketball coach at Greene County for a while.

But Coach Whitehead probably made his biggest mark on the students as a chemistry and science teacher.

"Mr. Whitehead was a fantastic chemistry teacher," said Tom Faust, who was a junior in the 1970–1971 school year. "I learned so much from him." Nathaniel Whitehead died from cancer on September 10, 2004.

Coach Nathaniel Whitehead was an outstanding girls' basketball coach, track coach, and chemistry teacher. Photo courtesy of Greene County High School.

Ford Boston, Superintendent of Schools

Ford Boston, the Greene County superintendent of schools, worked behind the scenes with educators such as William Breeding to make the transition to full integration as smooth as possible. Photo courtesy of Greene County High School.

Harry Ford Boston came to Greene County in 1948 as a vocational instructor. He was appointed superintendent of schools on December 7, 1955, after the death of then-superintendent Floyd T. Corry in an automobile accident.

Mr. Boston was known as someone who took great pride in the accomplishments of Greene County's students.

"Mr. Boston came up to me after our spring game and said, 'You sure did throw some pretty passes today,'" said Charles Turner. "That he would take the time to talk to me gave me a lot of confidence."

Not long after I was hired by the *Atlanta Journal-Constitution* in 1984, I received a handwritten note from Mr. Boston saying how proud he was of me for representing Greene County.

"Daddy was always thinking about other people," said Elaine Boston Carsel, his daughter. "He took a lot of pride when Greene County students did well. He treated everybody the same."

Mr. Boston served as superintendent of the Greene County schools for twenty-nine years, retiring on January 1, 1985.

He died on July 25, 2004, at the age of ninety-one.

Ellis D. Foster, Principal

Principal Ellis Foster was a calm hand at the wheel as the new Greene County High School navigated the sometimes-choppy waters of integration. He left for a job in Hart County after the 1970–1971 academic year. Photo courtesy of Greene County High School.

Ellis Foster was affectionately known by his friends as "Fess," but you would never hear that name used by the students, who respected him immensely.

He was born in Darien, Georgia, and attended Piedmont College. After military service, he received a degree from the University of Georgia and began his career in education. In 1949 he came to Greensboro High School, where he taught English and English literature and coached boys' basketball.

In 1959, he was named principal of Greensboro High School. In 1965, the high schools in Greensboro and Union Point merged to form Greene County High School. Mr. Foster was named principal of the new school.

When Greene County High School and Floyd T. Corry merged in 1970, Mr. Foster was named principal. Taking over a new school going through integration would be one of the biggest challenges of his career.

Mr. Foster devoted twenty-three years of his life to being a teacher, coach, and principal in the high schools of Greene County.

"Mr. Foster was a calm and collected leader," said Christine West, his administrative assistant. "You always felt he had things under control."

But let's be clear on this. Despite his outwardly composed manner, Mr. Foster liked to win, whether it was on the football field, the basketball court, or the golf course.

He also believed there was educational value in getting outside the walls of the school.

"I remember him sending me a note to come to his office," said Coach Poss. "I was going to be coaching girls' basketball, and he said, 'Get yourself a substitute for the next two days. Our basketball coaches need to go to Macon to see the state tournament.'"

For those students who loved golf, he had a deal: if we could get tickets to the Masters golf tournament in Augusta (only about an hour away), we could skip school to attend. Eric Ashley landed a couple of tickets in 1970. We showed Mr. Foster the tickets, and he said, "Go!"

On March 15, 1971, Mr. Foster tendered his resignation to the Greene County School Board.

He later took a position as principal of Hart County Junior High School in Hartwell. Greene County had been the only home his daughters Kathie and Sandy and their brother, Phil, had ever known. Kathie was a junior at Greene County High School when it merged with Floyd T. Corry.

The day he resigned, she said, "was a very tough day. Daddy always did what was best for the family, and he thought this would be the best move for my younger sister's education. He was ready for another challenge."

Mr. Foster later became the Hartwell city manager, a post he held for eighteen years.

"He dabbled in real estate a little, was a locksmith, made wine," said Kathie. "He had a lot of interests."

Mr. Foster passed away on June 30, 2008. Two years later, on December 16, 2010, his wife, Elaine Hunt Foster, passed away.

Kathie and her husband, Eddie McCurley, still live in Hartwell.

"With my dad, you always knew where you stood," said Kathie. "He was honest, and he was very loyal. He was a wonderful father to us, as well as a mentor to players and students who were fortunate enough to have known him."

Christine West, Administrative Assistant

Christine West was not only Mr. Foster's longtime administrative assistant but also a friend to a generation of Greene County High School students. In fact, the 1968 senior class dedicated the school yearbook to her.

When Mr. Foster left Greene County, Evans Acree came in as principal and brought his wife with him as his administrative assistant.

Mrs. West then worked at Nathanael Greene Academy, and today she is an administrative assistant at the First Baptist Church in Greensboro.

Christine West, longtime administrative assistant to Principal Ellis Foster, was beloved by Greene County students. Photo courtesy of Greene County High School.

Eli Jackson was the beloved principal at Floyd T. Corry High School when it merged with Greene County High School in 1970. Photo courtesy of Greene County High School.

Eli Jackson was one of the most decorated educators in the history of the state of Georgia. Having completed his course of study at the Tuskegee Normal and Industrial Institute in 1928, he was encouraged to go into teaching by his friend, Leroy Johnson, a successful real estate executive, and his mother, Birdie Jackson.

He began his career as the teacher and principal of a one-teacher school in Oglethorpe County, Georgia. After some time on the family farm, where he helped his mother by farming and teaching his younger brothers and sisters, he came to Greene County in 1933 to serve as principal of a school for African American children in Woodville.

He married his wife, Elsie, in 1937, and they both took teaching jobs at the Maxeys Lodge High School in Oglethorpe County, beginning a long life together as a teaching team. According to his obituary, Mr. Jackson would not take a job unless there was a position available for his wife.

In 1951, Greene County school superintendent Floyd T. Corry arranged for Mr. Jackson to take over as principal of the Greensboro High School for Negroes, which subsequently became known as Greene County High School. The county's predominately white school was Greensboro High School.

Five years later, Greene County High School would be renamed when Mr. Corry was killed in an automobile crash.

In 1970, Mr. Jackson accepted the job as associate principal at Greene County High School. In May 1970, he was honored with a special appreciation event at Floyd T. Corry, which would graduate its final senior class before merging with Greene County High School that fall.

According to his obituary, "Mr. Jackson was a caring person and principal for more than 41 years, which enabled him to be an influential role model for many young men and women throughout this region. He was a warm, loving, joyful Christian with a radiant smile."

He passed away on February 22, 1992.

His wife, Elsie Hopson Jackson, served as his secretary and was by his side for fifty-seven years. She passed away on December 22, 2003.

"I will never forget Mr. Jackson," said Charles Turner, who attended Corry up until his senior year of high school. "He was a father figure to everybody. My family was close to him because of my mom. He recruited her as a teacher. He was incredibly supportive of all students. Without Mr. Jackson there is no Floyd T. Corry High."

Today Greene County's educational complex is named for Eli J. Jackson, Floyd T. Corry, and Ford Boston, who succeeded Corry as the superintendent of schools.

Tommi Ward

Almost all of us remember a teacher who made a real difference in our lives. This teacher was a source of inspiration, confidence, and encouragement to be the very best you could be.

For me, that teacher was Tommi Ward.

Tommi was twenty-one years old when she graduated from North Georgia College (now University of North Georgia), where she is in the school's Alumni Hall of Fame. In fact, sixteen members of her direct family have attended North Georgia.

Her father, Brigadier General Hughes L. Ash, and his wife, Minnie Louise Ash, had moved to Greene County after the general had retired from the military.

Tommi Ward was only twenty-one years old when she came to Greene County High School to teach English in the fall of 1969. Photo courtesy of Greene County High School.

In 1969, Tommi's husband, Rick, was sent to Vietnam.

"So my parents said come back here [to Greene County] and teach and live with us. So I did," Tommi said.

Little did Tommi Ward know that her first teaching assignment would be historic.

Prior to the start of the 1969–1970 school year, the decision was made to teach fully integrated English classes at Floyd T. Corry High, a predominately African American school. White students would be bused to Corry from nearby Greene County High. This would serve as an interim measure before full integration of the two schools began in the fall of 1970.

It was a tough time for Tommi. Each day, with equal parts hope and dread, she would look at the *Atlanta Constitution* newspaper to check the names of those killed or wounded in Vietnam.

"I did it every single day," she said.

In February 1970, she was in school when suddenly an inexplicable feeling came over her.

"I just had a feeling that something was not right," she said. She went to the office of Principal Ellis Foster and said she needed to go home.

"Then I burst into tears," she said.

When she turned the corner onto her street, Tommi saw her parents in the driveway. With them was Ray Marchman, who ran the local office for Western Union.

He had a telegram.

Rick had been wounded, but he was going to be okay.

In April 1971, Tommi left Greene County to rejoin Rick, who had returned from Vietnam and was stationed at Fort Bragg, North Carolina. She came back for our graduation.

When Rick got out of the army in 1974, he and Tommi moved back to Greene County, where she served as an English teacher at Nathanael Greene Academy for thirty-five years. Tommi and Rick still live in Greene County.

William J. Breeding

Mr. Breeding served the Greene County School System for more than forty years as a teacher, principal, and coach. He did so without missing a single day of work.

He was educated in the schools of Birmingham, Alabama, and went on to receive his undergraduate degree at Clark College before earning advanced degrees from Atlanta University and the University of Georgia.

As an educator, he was invited to the White House by both President Jimmy Carter and President Bill Clinton. Three different Georgia governors appointed him to various state commissions.

According to his obituary, he was a mainstay in educational, civic, political, economic, and religious affairs in Greene County.

As the girls' basketball coach at Floyd T. Corry High School, he won state championships in 1959, 1960, and 1962.

What is not well known is how many people Mr. Breeding helped financially so they could go to college.

William Breeding was a lifelong educator who was honored by the Georgia legislature when he passed away in March 2006. Mr. Breeding also won three state championships as a girls' basketball coach. Photo courtesy of Katrina Breeding.

"He loved education and helping kids to get an education," said his daughter, Katrina, who is an attorney in Greensboro. "What I like about my dad is he put his money where his mouth was. He cared for other people's kids as if they were his own."

When Mr. Breeding passed away in March 2006, the Georgia State House of Representatives passed a resolution honoring his career in education. The resolution was sponsored by Representative Mickey Channell of the 116th district (which includes Greene County) and Representative Tyrone Brooks of the 63rd district.

11

LESSONS I LEARNED ABOUT RACE

In the winter of 2022, I was putting the final touches on this book. At that point, I was satisfied that I had handled the major themes—football, politics, and race in small-town Georgia—with equal parts sensitivity and realism.

The subject of race, as I wrote in the introduction, had to be addressed in this book. And from my perspective, which is that of a sixty-nine-year-old white man, the first year of full integration at Greene County High School (1970–1971) went well.

While doing the interviews for this book, I found that my African American teammates—Charles Turner, Guy Crutchfield, Ben Allen Gresham, Arthur Jackson, Mike Jackson, James Kimbro—were, to a man, complimentary about how the year was handled.

Did everything go perfectly?

"No. We had our difficult moments, but we worked through them," said Arthur Jackson. "But we had good people on our team and in our new school who wanted it to work. I have absolutely no regrets."

And in the telling of this story, we should never forget that our African American classmates had to leave their high school, Floyd T. Corry, and all its great traditions and memories to merge with Greene County and form a new school.

Bottom line: the black students in the 1971 senior class of Greene County High School made the biggest sacrifice—one that

I don't think I fully appreciated at the time. Hopefully this book will make us all more aware of what they gave up to help us all move forward as a school, as a community, and as a country.

But in 2020, while we continued to battle the COVID-19 virus, events took place that had people of good conscience taking a second look at the reality of day-to-day life for people of color in this country.

The death of George Floyd at the hands of Minneapolis police in May 2020 and that of Breonna Taylor in Louisville in March of that year sparked nationwide discussion that challenged us all to do some real soul-searching about race in our country.

I ultimately decided that I couldn't end this book—which has been a wonderful journey that few people get to have in their lives—without dealing with this most uncomfortable subject.

The first call I made was to our quarterback, Charles Turner.

If there is a hero in this book, it is Charles. It was Charles who showed the leadership that was necessary not only for our African American teammates but for the rest of the team as well. Without Charles Turner showing the way, I don't think the full integration of the 1970 Greene County football team—or of the entire school—would have been as successful as it was.

"I knew the guys kind of looked up to me and depended on me for a lot of advice and help," he said.

And it wasn't just the football players. All of the students who came to Greene County High from Corry High followed Charles's lead.

"He was a godsend," said Nicholas Antone, our African American English teacher and assistant football coach. "I can't think of anybody during that era who would have made the transition go as smoothly as he did.

"Everybody knew how good he was athletically. But he had the entire package mentally and academically. He was admired wherever he went. I've been here [in Greene County] for over fifty years. Charles is the best athlete I have seen."

He also became my first African American friend.

I still remember when the final seconds ticked off the clock of our last game at Gainesville on November 20, 1970. As I walked off the field, the first teammate I encountered was Charles. He stuck out his hand.

"Thanks for everything," he said.

Actually, I needed to thank Charles at that moment because I learned a lot more from him and my African American teammates that fall than they learned from me. In many ways, being a member of the 19 of Greene started my own personal journey of learning about and dealing with the realities of life faced by people of another race.

Before I played for the 19 of Greene, I never really thought about race. That's because I didn't have to.

After we left Greene County High School in the spring of 1971, Charles and I stayed in touch off and on over the years.

When I had the idea of doing this book, the first phone call I made was to Charles. If he didn't embrace the idea, it was not going to happen.

We met for lunch in Athens. I brought the team photo that is on the cover of this book and basically outlined the entire project. Sixteen of the nineteen members of our team were still alive, and I would need his help in tracking some of them down. After all, it had been almost fifty years since he or I had seen many of them.

He immediately approved. In fact, while we were at lunch, we called several teammates and told them about the book. To a man, they were all excited. This was an opportunity to relive that season, something many of us thought we would never do.

On October 17, 2019, Charles and I met for the first of several interviews for this book. He was returning from a meeting of the Georgia Athletic Directors Association and came to my home in Dunwoody, Georgia.

I told Charles that day that an important part of this book would be dealing with the subject of race. This was the story of nineteen high school students—twelve white, seven black—who formed a team within the external pressures of integrating the entire school.

Race—and people's feelings about race—had to be in the book.

And I needed Charles to help educate me on race so that I could write about it. He said he wouldn't hold anything back.

Charles said his views on race and civil rights began with Dr. Martin Luther King Jr., President John F. Kennedy, and Robert Kennedy. He was only ten years old when President Kennedy was assassinated in 1963. He was fifteen when Dr. King and Robert Kennedy were assassinated in 1968.

"They were idols of mine," he said.

He told me the story of being pulled over by the police in the backwoods of Comer, Georgia, in the 1970s. They screamed at him because he HAD NOT been drinking. He was scared.

"I really thought I was going to lose my life that night," he said.

But they let him go. Charles had done what his father told him to do in any encounter with the police: remain calm and cooperate.

I would learn that in the African American community it is called "The Talk."

My dad never had that talk with me. He didn't need to.

Charles and his wife, Cynthia, raised two sons and a daughter and educated them on the realities of being a young black person in America.

"There is still a lot of injustice in the world," he said. "But what I told them is that you have to make your own way in life. Don't ever expect people to give you anything. You have to earn everything that you get. That is what my parents taught me, and I passed it along to my children and grandchildren."

There are still many changes that we must make before we can call this a truly just society. Justice is not a destination but an ongoing journey. Those of us who grew up without the daily burden of dealing with race have to start doing the heavy lifting here. People like Charles and my African American teammates at Greene County High School have had to handle this burden for too long.

And the hope is that the process of change—meaningful and lasting change—is now beginning.

"I'm mature enough to understand that it's still not truly a level playing field," Charles said. "I was taught to be respectful of others. I expect them to be respectful of me."

Charles was working at a manufacturing plant in Union Point in the summer after his freshman year at Clark College.

"I got to see how people [of color] were treated," he said. "I saw the way the real world worked. I noticed who the laborers were and who the supervisors were. You weren't treated the same.

"That summer I told myself, 'You will graduate from college.'"

He graduated from Clark College in four years.

When Charles and I talked about this subject, we had to admit that our nation is more divided now than at any time since the Civil War.

But I was also impressed by the fact that despite our nation's problems, despite our failure at times to live up to the promise of equal protection under the law as a society, Charles still believes in the fundamental goodness of America.

"We are all human beings. Right is right, and wrong is wrong. We all know that. It's not complicated," he said. "But the fact is that this is still America, and I'd rather be in America than anywhere else. I am blessed in a lot of ways."

If Charles Turner still feels blessed to be an American, then so should we all. But we also should rededicate ourselves to making sure the blessings of this great country are available to all and to working continually to bring down the barriers to full participation in this great experiment in freedom we call the United States of America.

The year was 2009. I was working on a television show called *Talkin' Football* for css, a cable sports network owned by Comcast. During a break in the taping, a young cameraman walked over to the desk. He looked familiar.

"Mr. Barnhart, my name is Curtis Turner," he said. "I think you know my father."

"Yes I do," I told Charles Turner's youngest son. "He taught me a lot."

FANNIE PEAKS: IF YOU CUT US, WE ALL BLEED THE SAME BLOOD

I reached out to a couple more friends in Greene County to get their take on race relations in the county, past and present.

Fannie Peaks became my senior classmate at Greene County High School when it merged with her school, Floyd T. Corry, in the fall of 1970.

Fannie grew up in the Canaan section of Greensboro, in an area known as "The Alley." She was one of twelve children (six boys, six girls) born to Willie and Odessa Peaks.

"Momma said that she would take charge of the girls, and he [her father] would discipline the boys," said Fannie, when we met at Festival Hall on January 28, 2022. "My momma and daddy didn't play. We were disciplined."

Odessa Peaks had one hard and fast rule: the children did not leave "The Alley" and go to other parts of Canaan or to the projects without her permission.

While things were difficult for her family in the 1950s and 1960s, today Fannie looks back at those times as being some of the best in her life.

"While I was growing up, it seemed like it was so hard," she said. "It seemed like my parents were always struggling to make ends meet. But we always had food, we always had clean clothes, and we always had a clean house."

On those very warm summer nights in Georgia, Fannie remembered that her mother would pull the mattresses out onto the front porch, where they would sleep.

"We didn't have air conditioning," she said. "But we were never afraid."

Fannie said her father tended to five gardens in Canaan.

"Daddy would share what he had. If somebody needed something, he would tell them to go to the garden and get it," she said.

When it came to race relations, Odessa Peaks was clear with her children. She had worked at Caldwell's Laundry and Dry Cleaning, a white-owned business, for years until her health forced her to quit in 1969. In that capacity, she interacted with white people on a daily basis. Willie Peaks worked at the Greensboro water department.

"My mom instilled in us that there was only one God. And if you cut us, we bleed the same blood," she said.

Fannie has written and published a daily devotional book, *From Your Pain to God's Promise.*

TRUDY MCCOMMONS: THE ANSWER IS ALWAYS "YES"

On that same trip to see Fannie, my wife, Maria, and I visited Pauline Channell, Maria's 103-year-old aunt.

While in downtown Greensboro, we stopped to visit Trudy McCommons, whose family owns one of the funeral homes in Greene County.

Maria's mother, Catherine, and Trudy's mother, Rachel, were lifelong friends. I grew up in Union Point and went to school with Trudy and her brothers and sisters.

Trudy attended Greene County High School and graduated in 1968, two years before the school would totally integrate. She married Steve McCommons, who graduated in 1967. The McCommons family has owned the funeral home for five generations. Steve and Trudy also own a gift shop in downtown Greensboro.

As the owner of two businesses that deal with a diverse group of people every single day, Trudy said she understood the importance of respecting all races.

Trudy mentioned that over the years, black members of the community have reached out to her to ask, "When I die, will your funeral home take care of me?"

The concern expressed in their question is whether a "white" funeral home would be willing to handle the arrangements for a black person. The answer, said Trudy, has always been, "Of course we will."

Trudy told us of an interracial couple—he was black and she was white—who wanted to know if McCommons would take care of the husband when he passed. The answer, Trudy said, is always "yes."

Trudy's point? While McCommons Funeral Home has had many black clients over the years, there is still concern among people of color about prejudice in the white community of Greensboro. This concern is certainly real, but there is also hope that at the core there are citizens who rise above this prejudice and treat all people with dignity and respect.

That's what Trudy and Steve have done with their business.

Not everything that is faced can be changed. But nothing can be changed until it is faced.—**JAMES BALDWIN**

EPILOGUE

We, the staff of the 1971 *Tiger*, dedicate this yearbook to the spirit maintained by Greene County High School during the transitional year of public education. We salute our faculty and students who have kept our spirit alive, always remembering that no student should be deprived of an opportunity for education.—Dedication from the Greene County High School 1970–1971 yearbook

A lot has changed in Greene County in the fifty-plus years since the 19 of Greene played their final game together.

In 1979, the Georgia Power Company completed construction on the Wallace Dam, which harnessed the Oconee River and created Lake Oconee, bringing 374 miles of beautiful shoreline to Greene, Morgan, and Putnam Counties.

Lake Oconee has become one of the great resort areas in the United States. It is home to some of the best golf courses in the country, lake resorts filled with million-dollar homes, and an expanding tax base that has helped the county as a whole.

Until 2007, high-school-age students in Greene County had only two options: Greene County High School and Nathanael Greene Academy (NGA), a private school founded in 1969. NGA began with an enrollment of 189 in grades 1–12; its first graduating class in 1970 had only 5 students.

That dynamic changed with the building of Lake Oconee Academy in 2007. The charter school began with only a handful

161

of students; today it has more than one thousand students in grades K–12.

Charter schools are public schools that use public funds but are not subject to all state regulations. Instead, they agree to uphold a set of performance standards, or charters, that have been negotiated with the state. Teachers are given more flexibility to create programs to fit their students' needs. Charter schools must follow state law when it comes to discrimination by race or national origin.

Lake Oconee Academy (LOA) has been an unqualified success for its students. According to the Governor's Office of Student Achievement (GOSA), the academy's overall performance is higher than that of 70 percent of the schools in Georgia.

According to the most recent figures available from GOSA, in the 2020–2021 school year LOA's student body (K–12) was 68 percent white, 12 percent black, and 12 percent Hispanic.

By comparison, of the 442 students enrolled in grades 9–12 at Greene County High School, approximately 73 percent were black, 14 percent were Hispanic, and 11 percent were white, according to GOSA. (In the spring of 1971, the first fully integrated senior class at Greene County High School comprised fifty-seven black and fifty-six white students.) Meanwhile, Nathanael Greene Academy reports that its student body in the current (2022–2023) school year—ninety-three students—is roughly 95 percent white and 4 percent black.

Dr. Otho Tucker, who has been the CEO of Lake Oconee Academy since it opened, said that diversity among LOA's faculty and student body is something "we're aware of and something we continue to address."

But options to expand the academy's minority enrollment are limited.

Each year there is a lottery for the limited slots available. The lottery is open to all residents of Greene County.

By Georgia law, preference is given to children of members of the LOA governing board, children of school employees, and siblings of current students. Preference is also given to children who matriculate from a prekindergarten program that is associated with the school.

After all the slots were filled by the lottery for the 2020–2021 school year, there were still 336 children on the waiting list.

Proponents of Lake Oconee Academy insist that another educational opportunity was needed to attract younger families to Greene County.

Critics believe that, despite the academy's success, the county's schools are again segregated by race.

And the emotional temperature of this debate was not lowered by the fact that the LOA Board of Governors filed a lawsuit against the Greene County Board of Education in September 2020. According to a report in the *Lake Oconee News* on December 22, 2022, the lawsuit claimed that the Greene County BOE was violating the LOA state charter by not fully funding the school. Specifically, the disagreement was over how many students the LOA charter allows the academy to enroll and how many should be funded by the Greene County BOE. On January 26, 2023, the *Lake Oconee News* and the *Herald-Journal* both reported that the two parties had reached a settlement. As part of the settlement, the Greene County School District will pay the LOA just under $1.1 million over six years.

More than fifty years after the 19 of Greene helped rally a community that was going through the historic change of integration, what is the significance of the recent enrollment figures for LOA, NGA, and Greene County High School?

Do those numbers mean that after five decades, we're back to where we started on the subject of race and education?

We'll leave that question for the historians to decide.

As a former coach once told me, when it comes to sensitive subjects like this, "Where you stand depends on where you sit."

David Kopp is a lifelong resident of Greene County who came home after earning a law degree at the University of Georgia in 1974 and set up his practice in Greensboro. He has had a front-row seat for everything that has happened in Greene County over the past five decades.

Kopp concedes that the issue of Lake Oconee Academy has been controversial.

"Like most things in life, it's not all good and not all bad," said Kopp, whose father was a Baptist minister. "But I do know this: we were put on this earth to work together."

Lately, the news on education in Greene County has been very good. In June 2022, the county broke ground on a brand-new, state-of-the-art elementary school. It should open in July 2023.

According to Principal Eddie Hood, Greene County High School's graduation rate in 2020 was 91.6 percent. In 2021, it was 86.5 percent.

"The good news is that we're graduating our kids, but my focus as a first-year principal is to just get them prepared to be productive citizens after high school," said Hood.

The Thillen Education Foundation, which was created in 1999 and is dedicated to matching high school students with career coaches and professionals in their chosen field, set a goal of raising $1 million within a year's time to underwrite the program at Greene County High School's College and Career Academy. This academy not only prepares students for college but also gives students a wide range of vocational options that includes culinary arts, cosmetology, and agriculture mechanics, just to name a few.

The foundation met its goal in only four months.

WE CELEBRATED OUR FIFTIETH ANNIVERSARY ON ZOOM

On September 27, 2019, my wife, Maria, and I attended homecoming at Greene County High School, where I joined four of my 1970 teammates—Charles Turner, Mike Jackson, Al Cason, and Dene Channell.

We celebrated the forty-ninth anniversary of our 1970 team and promised each other that, God willing, many more of us would be back for the fiftieth in 2020.

Unfortunately, that was not possible.

The COVID virus was still very much part of our existence when the 2020 football season started. Limits on crowds, mask

Because of COVID, the 19 of Greene had to celebrate their fiftieth anniversary on Zoom. The call lasted for over ninety minutes. Photo courtesy of Tony Barnhart.

requirements, and social distancing policies were still in place. And the reality was that we were all now in the most vulnerable age group when it came to the virus.

Thus we couldn't have our anniversary celebration in person.

So the 19 of Greene had its fifty-year reunion on November 10, 2020, via Zoom. Seven players—Charles Turner, Tommy Faust, Arthur Jackson, Al Cason, Dene Channell, Charles Martin, and myself—were joined by three coaches—Dennis Fordham, Nicholas Antone, and Mack Poss.

The call was scheduled to last forty-five minutes. We were laughing so hard and having so much fun that the call went on for more than an hour and a half.

Charles Turner, of course, put it all together. After all, he's still our quarterback.

While COVID wiped out the 2020 and 2021 homecoming celebrations at Greene County High School, we will never forget that 2019 homecoming at Tiger Stadium. My wife—also a native of Greene County, and my high school sweetheart—and I were welcomed back by my classmates and teammates, most of whom I had not seen since graduation day in 1971.

Each graduating class from Greene County High School had its own tent. The 1971 tent, designed by Charles Turner's sports marketing business, featured large photos of Eli and Elsie Jackson; William J. Breeding; Felton Hudson, one of Charles's most influential teachers; and Charles's parents, Charlie and Chloe Turner.

"It's just my way of respecting the important people who have come before me," Charles said.

In the distance, up the hill from the football stadium, we could see the old gymnasium where we were graduated almost fifty years ago. But we didn't talk about the political or sociological implications of what we had done together in the fall of 1970.

We didn't talk about being trailblazers and helping a community rally around a special team and a special time in our history.

We talked about football, our children, and our grandchildren.

We talked about that cold, rainy, muddy, godforsaken night in Gainesville, when our little band of nineteen players stood toe-to-toe with one of the best teams in the state. Yes, Gainesville won the game, but when it was over, the Red Elephants knew they had been in a helluva fight.

About an hour before kickoff, we joined alumni from other Greene County classes to form a human corridor for the 2019 Greene County Tigers as they made their way into the stadium. They went out and beat Georgia Military College (49–9) for their first win of the season.

Tommi Ward, the courageous twenty-one-year-old English teacher who in the fall of 1969 led an uncertain group of white children to Floyd T. Corry to take English and to pave the way for full integration in 1970, was there to hug her former students.

Tommi was the teacher who convinced me that I could be a writer for a living. The fall of 2023 marked my forty-seventh year of covering college football, and Tommi remains one of my biggest supporters.

Nicholas Antone, who, along with Barbara Christian, welcomed students from Greene County High to Floyd T. Corry in the fall of 1969, was also there.

I hugged my teammates and classmates. We took pictures together and laughed. Man, did we laugh.

Had it really been fifty years?

The wrinkles and the gray hair and the stiff joints and the waistlines most certainly said "yes."

But for that one night, in our minds and in our hearts, the 19 of Greene were young again. Despite the passage of time, we were ready to run onto the field at Tiger Stadium one more time and do what nobody thought we could do.

We were a team of black men and white men for which the whole—in football and in life—was so much greater than the sum of its parts. Despite all that has happened, that is just as true today as it was fifty years ago.

When it was over, we all looked forward to the day when we could have homecoming at Greene County High School again.

It finally happened in 2022.

THE LAST WORD: CHARLES TURNER IS INDUCTED INTO THE GREENE COUNTY TIGERS RING OF HONOR

The phone call from Charles that day brought a good piece of news and a great piece of news.

The good news: after a two-year absence due to COVID, there would be another homecoming celebration at Greene County High School in October 2022.

The great news: Greene County High School was creating a "Tigers Ring of Honor" to recognize great players, coaches, and contributors of the past, and Charles would be among the first five people inducted.

It was a beautiful night at Tiger Stadium on October 7, 2022,

Charles Turner and his wife, Cynthia, their three children (Curtis, Chuck, Candace) and their six grandchildren (Christopher, Cassius, Harper Claire, Camryn, Turner Rose, Chase) as Charles is inducted into Greene County High School's first Ring of Honor on October 7, 2022. On the far left is GCHS principal Eddie Hood. On the far right is athletic director Derrick Williams. Photo courtesy of Beth Lyon.

and the ladies of our 1971 graduating class prepared a wonderful meal for our tailgating experience.

Charles and Cynthia brought their three adult children and six grandchildren. They were all on the field together when Charles received the award.

Five of Charles's fourteen living teammates also came to support him: Al Cason, Arthur Jackson, Dene Channell, Ricky Easley, and me.

"I can't tell you how much it meant to have you guys here," Charles said after the ceremonies. "We've all come a long way together."

Yes, we have. Since the spring of 1970, when we began to put our team together, each of us, by the grace of God, has lived fifty-two years bonded by this common and unforgettable experience. And whatever awaits us in the time we have left on this earth, we are, and will always be, the 19 of Greene.

That, and the wonderful memories that go with it, can never be taken away from us.

And brothers and sisters, it doesn't get any better than that.

Editor's note: On September 29, 2023, Tony Barnhart joined Charles Turner as a member of the Greene County Tigers Ring of Honor. He was inducted during ceremonies before the Homecoming game at Tiger Stadium.

Charles Turner with four of his 1970 Greene County teammates just moments after he was inducted into the Tigers Ring of Honor. (L-R) Tony Barnhart, Al Cason, Charles Turner, Arthur Jackson, and Dene Channell. Ricky Easley also attended the ceremony. Photo courtesy of Tony Barnhart.